DIGITAL
MAVERICKS

DIGITAL MAVERICKS

A GUIDE TO WEB3, NFTs, AND BECOMING THE MAIN CHARACTER OF THE NEXT INTERNET REVOLUTION

DEBBIE SOON

WILEY

Copyright © 2025 by John Wiley & Sons, Inc. All rights reserved, including rights for text and data mining and training of artificial technologies or similar technologies.

Published by John Wiley & Sons, Inc., Hoboken, New Jersey.
Published simultaneously in Canada.

No part of this publication may be reproduced, stored in a retrieval system, or transmitted in any form or by any means, electronic, mechanical, photocopying, recording, scanning, or otherwise, except as permitted under Section 107 or 108 of the 1976 United States Copyright Act, without either the prior written permission of the Publisher, or authorization through payment of the appropriate per-copy fee to the Copyright Clearance Center, Inc., 222 Rosewood Drive, Danvers, MA 01923, (978) 750-8400, fax (978) 750-4470, or on the web at www.copyright.com. Requests to the Publisher for permission should be addressed to the Permissions Department, John Wiley & Sons, Inc., 111 River Street, Hoboken, NJ 07030, (201) 748-6011, fax (201) 748-6008, or online at http://www.wiley.com/go/permission.

Trademarks: Wiley and the Wiley logo are trademarks or registered trademarks of John Wiley & Sons, Inc. and/or its affiliates in the United States and other countries and may not be used without written permission. All other trademarks are the property of their respective owners. John Wiley & Sons, Inc. is not associated with any product or vendor mentioned in this book.

Limit of Liability/Disclaimer of Warranty: While the publisher and author have used their best efforts in preparing this book, they make no representations or warranties with respect to the accuracy or completeness of the contents of this book and specifically disclaim any implied warranties of merchantability or fitness for a particular purpose. No warranty may be created or extended by sales representatives or written sales materials. The advice and strategies contained herein may not be suitable for your situation. You should consult with a professional where appropriate. Further, readers should be aware that websites listed in this work may have changed or disappeared between when this work was written and when it is read. Neither the publisher nor authors shall be liable for any loss of profit or any other commercial damages, including but not limited to special, incidental, consequential, or other damages.

For general information on our other products and services or for technical support, please contact our Customer Care Department within the United States at (800) 762-2974, outside the United States at (317) 572-3993 or fax (317) 572-4002.

Wiley also publishes its books in a variety of electronic formats. Some content that appears in print may not be available in electronic formats. For more information about Wiley products, visit our web site at www.wiley.com.

Library of Congress Cataloging-in-Publication Data

Names: Soon, Debbie (Businesswoman), author.
Title: Digital mavericks : a guide to Web3, NFTs, and becoming the main character of the next Internet revolution / Debbie Soon.
Description: Hoboken, New Jersey : Wiley, [2025] | Includes bibliographical references and index.
Identifiers: LCCN 2024028327 (print) | LCCN 2024028328 (ebook) | ISBN 9781394220892 (hardback) | ISBN 9781394220908 (adobe pdf) | ISBN 9781394233342 (epub)
Subjects: LCSH: NFTs (Tokens) | Blockchains (Databases) | Art and technology.
Classification: LCC HG1710.3 .S66 2025 (print) | LCC HG1710.3 (ebook) | DDC 332.4/048—dc23/eng/20240719
LC record available at https://lccn.loc.gov/2024028327
LC ebook record available at https://lccn.loc.gov/2024028328

Cover Design: Wiley
Cover Image: © Jamaali Roberts
SKY10093731_121824

Explore exclusive onchain experiences at **digitalmavericks.xyz**

Join our community of digital mavericks and unlock unique art collectibles inspired by the stories in this book.

To the dreamers who dare to do, and the doers who dare to dream:

This is our time.

Contents

Introduction — xi

Part 1   Viva la Revolución — 1

Chapter 1   Growing Up with the Internet — 3
Meet a Maverick: Randi Zuckerberg

Chapter 2   Taking Back Control — 17
Meet a Maverick: Foodmasku

Chapter 3   Of Sliced Bread and Paper — 31
Meet a Maverick: Jesse Pollak

Part 2   How to Become a Maverick — 47

Chapter 4   Step 1: Identify Your Glow Stick Moment — 49
Meet a Maverick: Latashá

Chapter 5	Step 2: Understand and Hold On to Your Why	63
	Meet a Maverick: Matt Medved and Alejandro Navia	
Chapter 6	Step 3: Get Your Hands Dirty	77
	Meet a Maverick: Shavonne Wong	
Chapter 7	Step 4: Transfer Your Skills	91
	Meet a Maverick: Jimena Buena Vida	
Chapter 8	Step 5: Join a Cabal . . . or Make Your Own	105
	Meet a Maverick: Zeneca	
Chapter 9	Step 6: Embrace the Chaos	119
	Meet a Maverick: Cozomo de' Medici	
Chapter 10	Step 7: Craft and Commit to a Ritual	133
	Meet a Maverick: Micah Johnson	
Part 3	**A New Era**	**149**
Chapter 11	The Robots Are Coming	151
	Meet a Maverick: Claire Silver	
Chapter 12	A Promised Land of False Starts	165
	Meet a Maverick: Li Jin	
Chapter 13	Diversity, Equity, and the Inclusiverse	177
	Meet a Maverick: Larisa Barbu	
Conclusion		*189*
Glossary		*193*
Notes		*201*

Resources	*207*
Acknowledgments	*213*
About the Author	*217*
Index	*219*

Introduction

It is the year 2018. The movie *Crazy Rich Asians* is released, becoming the most successful studio romantic comedy in nearly a decade at the US box office. Asians all over the world rejoice – after all, this is the first movie with an all-Asian cast coming out of Hollywood since 1993, and what a successful one at that.

For me, the movie quite literally hit home. Set in Singapore, *Crazy Rich Asians* was the first thing in the then-30 years of my life that gave the world a frame of reference for what it was like to live and grow up there. As heavily glamorized as the movie was, the picture it painted of Singapore was an undeniable improvement over what many others had until then assumed to be "some part of China."

The Singapore the world knows today resembles little of what I remember growing up in the '80s. Many landmarks that adorn our postcards (do people still send those anymore?) or tourism commercials were built in the last 10–15 years. In fact, I distinctly remember coming back for summer break while studying in college abroad, only to be completely taken aback by what looked like a spaceship perched precariously across three towering buildings. That architectural wonder turned out to be a Vegas-style integrated resort called Marina Bay Sands, and consisted of a casino, hotel, and shopping mall. It would later become a defining part of the city's skyline in years to come, with many of us forgetting that even the land it sits on was a result of man-made intervention (Figure 1).

Yet, as modern and technologically advanced Singapore appears to be, it still upholds socially conservative values, where free speech is considered a Western ideal and privilege that one chooses to pursue at their own peril. Locals are deterred from patronizing the aforementioned casino by being charged an entry levy, while the Singapore government has just started wrapping its head around the decriminalization of gay sex (same-sex marriage remains very much prohibited).

Figure 1 Marina Bay Sands.
Source: Hu Chen/UnSplash

Introduction xiii

I speak about Singapore so much partly because it has shaped so much of who I am – I was born and raised, and have established most of my career here, despite having since moved to Los Angeles after a pandemic-inspired move. But also because Singapore, a city-state of just 280 square miles with zero natural resources and a mere 59 years of history, epitomizes the spellbinding tension that has stemmed from a constant need to progress and innovate itself out of irrelevance.

Whether we know it yet, we as humans are in the crosshairs of a similar tension. In fact, we may very well be at the juncture of having to reinvent ourselves out of oblivion. The continued advances of blockchain[1] technology and now artificial intelligence (AI) represents a real threat that could easily render our place in the workforce, and by extension society, vulnerable. Yet, only a few of us are willing to confront that inevitability, let alone reflect upon our roles in that new reality – be that in the next 1, 5, or 10 years.

Those of us who do are what I like to refer to as mavericks – and more precisely, digital mavericks.

Today, I consider myself very much in the good company of fellow digital mavericks. Despite buying my first cryptocurrency[2] in the spring of 2019, it wasn't till the end of 2021 that I started getting intrigued about Web3 (a term used to describe a new evolution of the Internet powered by blockchain technology), and in particular non-fungible tokens[3] (NFTs). This was considered late by many – I wasn't an early collector of CryptoPunks or Bored Ape Yacht Club, nor did I really care to be. I was just intrigued by what I saw as an undeniable movement toward the purchasing, consuming, and owning of digital goods. After reading a *New York Magazine* article published in November 2021 titled "A Normie's Guide to Becoming

> *Taking risks, breaking the rules, and being a maverick have always been important but today they are more crucial than ever.*
> – Gary Hamel, American management consultant

a Crypto Person,"[4] I decided to get my feet wet by resurrecting my presence on X (formerly known as Twitter, and where the last tweet I had posted was probably in 2012), since that was where all the "crypto people" resided online.

According to the *New York Magazine* article, it was uncool to use my real name or my real photo on Twitter. I found and purchased an NFT of an avatar I liked – a witchy character with a crescent-shaped talisman and covetable long flowing black hair from an NFT collection called *Crypto Coven*. I also adopted the user handle safronova (Figure 2).

Safronova is actually the last name of a Russian volleyball player that I had seen once on TV during the 2004 Summer Olympics – liking how it sounded (it's a few letters away from the word supernova, which I was particularly fond of due to the song "Champagne Supernova" by British rock band Oasis), I ended up using it as a gaming handle in my teenage years. While I had not gamed for a while, it felt befitting to bring it back as a pseudonym

Figure 2   My very first NFT.

in an environment where it seemed many assumed alternate identities.

From there, I started to pen Twitter threads, sharing my learnings and takeaways about Web3, while also joining communities housed in Discord servers and making new friends over the Internet. It was in Discord that I met my now cofounder Randi Zuckerberg (as my witchy Internet self), the creator of Facebook Live as well as multiple-time Tony Award–winning Broadway producer – more on that later.

Together, we are building a company called HUG, a social platform for a new generation of blockchain-curious artists to showcase and sell their work (both on and off the blockchain), while connecting with each other and one-of-a-kind opportunities. Today, we are home to tens of thousands of artists across more than 160 different countries.

Through HUG, I am fortunate to work and interact with artists daily. Not only am I surrounded and inspired by creativity every single day, but I also get to see and experience firsthand how blockchain technology is evolving and creating new opportunities for these creators turned creative entrepreneurs.

Building on the front lines of Web3 is both empowering and lonely. There are days when it feels as if I am leading the charge in a revolution against Big Tech, seizing back control for the proletariat of everyday creators through the promise of true ownership. Most days, not only does the road ahead feel like June Gloom[5] in LA – most of the people in my personal life and even those I am advocating for (i.e. artists who have not yet dived into the world of NFTs) have little idea of what I do. "What the heck is an NFT anyway?" they say. "Isn't crypto just full of scammers?"

Like many other books written about Web3, *Digital Mavericks* is a time capsule, simply because of how much this space is about to evolve. That said, this is also an intentional snapshot of all the risk-takers who are making history as we speak.

There's a saying widely attributed to Winston Churchill that goes, "History is written by the victors." In my mind, that has never been a fair representation of what history is or should be (Mr. Miles, my high school history teacher, will be proud). Moreover, this characterization feels exceedingly unfair for something like Web3 – a technology, but more importantly a movement that is so deeply rooted in and driven by community. In fact, years down the road, my wish is for us to come out the other end fixated less on who's won and who's lost, but more so on what we have learned and on the change that we have fought for and inspired.

By the end of this book, I hope that you will have a deeper understanding of what Web3 is, why you should care, and why there are so many of us here breaking rules and challenging the status quo. More importantly, I also hope to convince you that you too have a place in this revolution if you choose to participate.

Do not get me wrong – Web3 is not perfect, be it the technology, the culture, how it is branded, and more. What I do know is that we are still early, yes – even in 2024, despite the first cryptocurrency (Bitcoin!) being created in 2009 and the first NFT being minted[6] (meaning, to be created on the blockchain) in 2014. I do not know about you, but I believe that anytime you are early to something is an opportunity to choose the role you would like to play, as well as shape the experience you'd like to have within it.

There is an equally high probability that after reading this you may think that Web3 and everything it entails (blockchain technology, crypto, NFTs, etc.) is not for you. You may even decide that you want nothing to do with it (even though my personal belief is that it will become ingrained in our lives without us realizing it). That's okay too.

Digital Mavericks is also meant to be an anthology – a collection of stories about everyday people like myself who have discovered a new sense of purpose and calling since encountering Web3. And while the whole idea of being on the cutting edge of emerging tech has been a huge part of that, I think you will realize that the one thing that has got us to this (at times cult-like) sense of wonder is the magical human connections we never thought possible.

Disclaimer: This book is anything but technical. In fact, I deliberately made it as nontechnical as possible. Not only are there far more qualified scholars on the subject of blockchain technology than me, but I also wanted this book to ultimately be approachable and to inspire further thought and action in even the most skeptical and unacquainted of readers.

To help you understand this new digital frontier, this book is split into three parts. The first, *Viva la Revolución*, is an introduction to what this Internet revolution even is. It provides history and context to how the Internet came to be, which if you are a millennial like me, will be like a trip down memory lane, before introducing you to Web3 through what are hopefully familiar concepts.

The second, *How to Become a Maverick*, is a step-by-step guide to how you can start to immerse yourself in this onchain world. Whether you are looking to eventually build a career here or are simply looking to become a more involved industry participant, here are my tips and tricks to help you stay grounded, survive the noise, and eventually thrive and find your true purpose.

The third and final part, *A New Era*, runs you through a few predictive trends I feel are worth highlighting and bracing yourself for. Because this space moves so fast, it is near impossible to make accurate forecasts of what will happen, and when. Nonetheless, I hope that these discussions will help you stay alert, and more importantly, get you excited about the role that you can play in shaping our digital future.

Along the way, you will also be introduced to several digital mavericks I've come to know and love. Some of them are artists, some are founders just like myself, others are community members and builders. While you may think every one of them crazy, you will notice that before Web3, the lives they led were nothing but relatable and dare I say it, normal. I hope that through their stories, you will be encouraged to take on risks of your own – to learn more and be curious about an industry that seems so incredibly foreign; to seek a career that aligns with your values and passions; and last but not least, to be open to picking up new skills in the advent of all the change that is about to confront us.

You see, Web3 should not be something that just happens to us. Instead, it should be a level playing field in which we get to take control of our own narrative, where we let our wants and needs determine what needs to be built, and how.

Welcome to *Digital Mavericks*, where the main character of the biggest Internet revolution our generation is about to see is none other than *you*.

PART 1

Viva la Revolución

You cannot buy the revolution. You cannot make the revolution. You can only be the revolution. It is in your spirit, or it is nowhere.
— Ursula K. Le Guin, American author

1

Growing Up with the Internet

I WAS BORN in 1988, putting me squarely in the middle of the generation we now term millennials. Millennials were the first generation to grow up with the Internet and then social media. It wasn't till years later that I realized this transition from my childhood into young adulthood also mirrored the evolution of the different phases of the Internet – and what we now term going from Web1 to Web2.

Web1 represents the early read-only version of the Internet. Back then, most people were passive consumers of information made available online. Website pages were static and gave users little way to interact with them. From a slightly more technical standpoint, content on website pages in Web1 were also hosted on the server's file system, as opposed to a relational database management system (RDBMS), which allows users to store, sort, and query information more easily.

Web1 was basically like taking a real-world dictionary, digitizing it, and making its content available for everyone to look at (but not react to) it online. From a timestamp perspective, I will also always associate Web1 with dial-up Internet, which in itself is embodied by a harrowing sound of nostalgia. More accurately, the cacophony of beeps and tones, which usually lasted around 19 seconds, was how long it took for us to access the World Wide Web.

Getting online was a scarce and prized event in my household growing up. Not only were Internet speeds painfully slow – it took around 20–30 minutes to download my favorite song by Christina Aguilera ("Genie in a Bottle," 1999) just so I could listen to it on demand and on repeat – but with the modem being connected to the phone lines, it also meant that anytime someone was connected to the Internet, our entire family would be incommunicado. Such was life before the dawn of mobile phones.

Yet, Web1 itself felt enticing enough at the time. Through a now-defunct MSN Messenger, we all got to talk to our newly met classmates and fifth-grade crushes, and then reinforce any budding friendships by recanting prior night conversations in class. Homework assignments felt easier too – asking Jeeves was a far quicker way of getting information than trying to navigate the Dewey decimal system in our school libraries.

Believe it or not, Web1 was the Internet I was familiar with all the way through graduating from high school. That said, as with anything, the move from Web1 to Web2 did not happen overnight, nor was it a result of a single discrete occurrence. In my teenage years, many of my peers and I dabbled in writing and putting out personal content on the Internet. We set up Livejournals and Tumblrs to share our teenage angst with strangers from across the world. It was exciting, nerve-racking, but also liberating. Those of us who were more adventurous went on to build personal websites on Geocities, before graduating to buying our very first domain names.

Then came Web2. Putting content and a little bit of ourselves into the world was now easier than ever. For me, the dawn of Web2 could not have come at a better time. I had just graduated from high school in the year 2006 and was presented with a life-changing opportunity to pursue a college education abroad through a scholarship from the Singapore government. I could not have been happier.

While I was filled with excitement about what this new chapter was about to bring (Independence! Freedom! New experiences!), it is never easy leaving friends, family, and everything you had ever known in life behind. Thankfully, the year 2006 also coincided with the year Facebook was made available to the general public. There was now an easy and what felt like a natural way to keep in touch with people from back home.

As I would soon come to learn, Facebook also made forming new friendships slightly easier in what would be a deeply unfamiliar and uncomfortable cultural environment (yes, the move from Singapore to the UK as an 18-year-old was not quite as easy as I thought it would be). Web2 gave rise to social networking, allowing us to build and maintain friendships with people from all around the world, while also facilitating the forming of digital communities based on shared interests and values.

The continued development of Web2, if we can even call it that, was simply an extension of the different ways in which humans connect and communicate. We went from text (Twitter) to photos (Instagram) to videos (YouTube, TikTok), where everyone could become a content creator in the medium they felt most comfortable. Those who were the earliest in embracing what Web2 could offer have gone on to become highly successful full-time content creators (or some may say, influencers), a career path which up until 15 years ago would have seemed completely made up.

Because the astronomic rise and penetration of Web2 occurred while I was in college, I never thought twice about what its significance was, let alone the role I could or should play in it. Not only was I studying for a degree in economics and hence more preoccupied with the implications of the global financial crisis, but I was also trying to figure out how to regulate my Asian flush so I could better fit in in a country with a heavy drinking culture.

Before I knew it, I, like many others, became just one of many passive users of the Web2 Internet. I mindlessly consume and react to the content that miraculously appears on my feed, I buy one too many things I do not need from the ads that I am served and in doing so, keep the wheels of the algorithm turning so it can keep doing what it does better.

Herein lies the pitfalls of Web2. While Web2 has delivered significant benefits to humankind, be it connecting long-lost friends or surfacing information we are seeking more quickly, it has done so at a price. "If you are not paying for the product, you are the product" is one of the most repeated quotes from Netflix documentary *The Social Dilemma*. Indeed, Web2 platforms have been able to become the most powerful advertisers the world has ever seen, by utilizing and selling the data and personal information we have so readily shared with them.

In the Internet revolution from Web1 to Web2, many of us have unwittingly played the role of what is now commonly known as a non-player character (NPC).[1] Compared to the early days of Web1, which was a new and novel way for everyday people to discover information and have fun, Web2 has to some extent taken that agency away by turning every single one of those activities into monetizable events.

Today, we are right at the cusp of another Internet revolution – from Web2 to Web3. And just like the previous revolution, this is a defining moment that will change how we interact, communicate, and collaborate, not just with each other but with brands, corporate entities, and even governments.

But Web3 is not just a technological innovation built on the backs of blockchain technology. It is also a cultural movement, in which many proponents and early builders in Web3 are viewing it as an opportunity to right the wrongs of Web2. After all, if Web2 companies are monetizing off the data and content that all of us have created, should we not also have the opportunity to monetarily benefit from what is fundamentally ours?

If Web1 was read-only, and Web2 is read and write, Web3 is a depiction of the Internet where we are able to read, write, and *own* our content. Web3 is about us, the everyday content creators, taking back control of what has been ours all along.

***

> **MEET A MAVERICK: How Randi Zuckerberg Is Setting Personal Records in the Race from Web2 to Web3**
>
> Randi Zuckerberg's unique background puts her at the forefront of both technology and media. As an early employee at Facebook and the creator of Facebook Live, she was on the front lines of shaping how billions of people consume content. Today, Randi is the founder and CEO of HUG, a social marketplace for next-generation creators to showcase and sell both onchain[2] and offchain[3] work. Randi is also an accomplished artist and producer who has performed on Broadway, won three Tony Awards, and hosts a weekly business talk radio show, *Randi Zuckerberg Means Business* on SiriusXM.

In April of 2024, Randi Zuckerberg had just competed in two out of six of the World Marathon Majors less than one week apart just a few weeks after recovering from a partially torn hamstring. She even achieved her second ever fastest marathon time of 3 hours, 37 minutes, and 5 seconds at the latter race at the London Marathon. Yet, the very next day, it was a different Zuckerberg that had made the headlines of *Runner's World* magazine.

While many of us may have experienced living in constant comparison to a family member (myself included), few will be able to understand what it's truly like when the family member in question is not only a household name but someone whose life's work has intimately transformed the way the entire world interacts with each other. In fact, as one of four children to a dentist father whose practice was located at the first floor of their house, Randi's childhood seemed remarkably normal aside from waking up regularly to the sounds of dental drills. "All four of us are pretty close in age, but we are such wildly different humans," Randi says about her siblings. "I was a drama nerd, Mark was into computers, and my two younger sisters were both really academic and sporty respectively . . . we were basically the Spice Girls if they were a family!"

For the longest time, musical theater was all Randi wanted to do. From the time she got gifted a Fisher Price record player at age two, Randi started singing and dancing to whomever would grant her an audience, and it would not take long before she started to more seriously rehearse and audition for performances at school. No matter how small the stage was at the time, performing imparted some valuable life lessons to Randi early on. She recalls a time when her mother made her demand for a solo at a choral recital in sixth grade even though no one had received one. "My mom was picking me up after practice and told me she would not move the car until I had gone back to ask for a solo," Randi says. "I was filled with so much anxiety, and even though it was so horrifically awkward, I asked my choir director Mr. Burke anyway." Randi ended up getting her first ever solo performance, and even though it was not more than 30 seconds, it taught her something she still believes in till today: if you do not ask for what you want, the answer will always be no.

Throughout high school, Randi continued to take her musical theater career aspirations seriously. She trained with an opera company and even got accepted into Juilliard, one of the world's most prestigious performing arts schools, whose alumni have won hundreds of any award you could think of from the Pulitzer Prize to the Oscars. Having also been accepted into Harvard and being faced with the decision of which school to attend, it was at this time when Randi first got served with a huge reality check from her music teacher. "He sat me down seriously and told me that I was not quite talented enough, and if I had a chance to go to Harvard, I should do that instead," Randi recalls. While that conversation hurt, it also felt surprisingly liberating. "I kind of already knew that I had hit a ceiling with what I could do in terms of pure talent," Randi says. "In some ways I felt relieved that I was now free to pursue other things."

It wasn't immediately clear to Randi what those other things were. "When you are a little girl, you often hear that you can have any job you want . . . as if it was something you could pick from a list of jobs that already existed," Randi tells me. "What no one ever tells you is that with entrepreneurship, you can actually create any job you want." Still, it would take a few years before Randi were to experience that possibility for herself. Instead, she fell in love with psychology classes at Harvard, where her classmates included renowned organizational psychologist Adam Grant and Oscar-winning actress Natalie Portman, and started to take an interest in business and marketing. "I got really intrigued by nature versus nurture and the emerging fields of positive and emotional psychology," Randi says. "Marketing felt like a way to apply these theories of why people do the things that they do in the real world."

Randi's first job out of college was in the Digital Marketing department of Ogilvy & Mather, a global advertising and brand agency. At the time though, that department felt more like a start-up housed within a large company. "I was actually pretty disappointed when I got staffed in that department," Randi laughs. "Especially when my other friends at Ogilvy were all working on glamorous television campaigns." Within a year, not only did Digital Marketing at Ogilvy end up becoming the company's most successful and fastest-growing team, but it also became the reason for a bunch of text messages she started to receive from her brother, Mark.

"My brother reached out to say, hey, I have this little start-up and could really use some advice from someone who understands digital marketing," Randi recalls. What was meant to be a brief consultation and weekend visit to Silicon Valley quickly turned into Randi negotiating a full-time offer to join her brother at Facebook. "Facebook was just a tiny office in Palo Alto with less than twenty people," Randi says. "Even then, I could tell that this small team truly believed that they were going to change the world and the way that we all communicated. They were working eighteen-hour days and yet seemed so happy."

What Randi saw was entrepreneurship in action. It quickly dawned upon her that by joining a start-up, she could be making strategic decisions at age 24 that shaped a company's trajectory, versus having to wait over 10 years in corporate America just to be let into the boardroom. "I was excited about the product and mission at Facebook, but I also saw it as a way for me to bypass a decade of my career," Randi says. Indeed, when Facebook started to field potential television and movie deals such as the 2010 film *The Social Network*, it came down to Randi to run the company's entire media operations. "Prior to joining Facebook, I had spent some time working on a TV series called *Forbes on Fox*," Randi tells me. "And because I was the only person in the company that had ever stepped onto a television set, I was asked to run that entire part of the business."

While at Facebook, Randi continued to work across several large projects, but perhaps none as influential as her work with Facebook Live. "When the iPhone first came out, I started to get really interested in the possibility of mobile live streaming," Randi recalls. "It wasn't even called live streaming at the time, but all I could think about was how we could each be our own media company if we were all holding something in the palm of our hands that had the computing power of a spaceship."[4] Initially conceived from a company hackathon, Facebook Live took years before becoming a commercially viable reality – its early iterations required large backpacks of equipment to simply be able to capture and then transmit live footage. Once it did however, it became home to not just celebrities such as Oprah Winfrey but also political figures such as President Obama. Randi ended up being nominated for an Emmy for Facebook's live coverage of the midterm elections in 2010.

While to onlookers it may have seemed that there could be no slowing Facebook down, it wasn't always a bed of roses. "The invention of the iPhone really freaked a lot of people out," Randi says. "In a few months, we went from 90% of our users using Facebook on a desktop to almost everyone switching their usage to mobile. None of our engineers had any experience with mobile, let alone the iPhone, since everything up until that point had been created from within Apple." Not knowing whether the iPhone and iOS were simply a fad or here to stay, Facebook made the decision to embrace the Apple ecosystem and train their engineers on it. "Betting on the iPhone turned out to be the right bet, but what if it had not worked out? We basically bet our entire company on it," Randi added.

Seven years into her career at Facebook, Randi eventually decided to take a different bet of her own, embracing motherhood and starting a family with her husband, Brent. "I was very pregnant during the Facebook Live broadcast with President Obama," Randi laughs. "We were also scheduled to do a Facebook Live with Hugh Jackman, whom I was absolutely obsessed with, when my water broke." Randi got rushed to the hospital to deliver her first son, Asher, and till today, has yet to meet the actor most famously known for playing Wolverine in the *X-Men* movies.

Cliché as it may sound, going on maternity leave and taking some time away from Facebook gave Randi an opportunity to properly examine where she was at in life. "Facebook had been such an incredible journey, and I had absolutely zero regrets about that experience," Randi says. "But I also realized I had spent almost an entire decade in service of someone else's dream as a supporting character." Ready for a leading lady role, Randi eventually stepped away from Facebook, opting instead to found her own production company, where she worked on a number of projects with varying degrees of success. While her first book with HarperCollins, *Dot Complicated*, ended up becoming a *New York Times* bestseller before getting turned into a children's animated series whose rights got acquired by Hulu, other endeavors such as a Bravo reality show called *Start-ups: Silicon Valley* were short-lived.

Regardless, Randi was having fun, this time with building her own company and not someone else's. A day after she found out that she was pregnant with her second child, the last thing Randi was expecting was to receive the call of her long forgotten teenage dreams. It was the Broadway musical *Rock of Ages*. "The producers called me to tell me that they were looking to do something crazy and have a tech personality star in their musical," Randi recalls. "I thought I was getting punked . . . I had given up on my dreams of being on Broadway so many years ago, and here I was at age thirty-two, getting a call in my living room asking me to perform on Broadway."

"Because I was pregnant, I told them I wanted to start immediately," Randi continues. "I received the call on a Thursday, and by Monday, I had moved to New York City to start rehearsing." Randi ended up playing Regina in *Rock of Ages* for a limited time run on Broadway, and while her stint on stage was brief, it was long enough to rekindle what Randi calls "the artist part of her soul."

After delivering her second child, Randi decided that returning to the stage was probably not the most sustainable path as a mother to two young children. Instead, she started to dip her toe into Broadway producing. "I got really interested in the business side of theater," Randi says. "It felt right up my alley after all my years working in Silicon Valley and business." Over the next couple of years, Randi went on to produce almost a dozen shows including Tony Award–winning musicals such as *Dear Evan Hansen*, *Hadestown*, and *Oklahoma*. Officially hooked and determined to continue making a name for herself in the Broadway scene, all of her dreams came crashing down with the onset of the pandemic in 2020.

"I remember thinking to myself, 2020 was going to be my year," Randi says. "Turns out 2020 was not my year . . . nor was it anyone else's." Broadway, along with the entire live events industry, ended up shutting down for 18 months. Till today, attendance remains below pre-pandemic levels.

Regardless, when one door closes, another opens. The name of the latter was Web3. "A few months into the pandemic, I started getting a lot of phone calls from venture capitalists who wanted me to advise them on deals in the NFT space," Randi recalls. "I did not really know much about NFTs, but these investors felt that my unique background of tech coupled with understanding the business of art would come in really handy in evaluating such deals." After seeing an entire billion-dollar industry get shuttered by government lockdowns, Web3 and all it offered in terms of the ability for artists to own and monetize their audiences felt like an alternate but far better reality.

"A world in which artists could control their destiny without being beholden to physical spaces or governments and other third parties telling them what to do is something I could not help but feel excited about," Randi says. Yet, Randi's personal onboarding to crypto did not go as smoothly as she would have liked. Within the first day of her adding her first Ethereum[5] (a cryptocurrency just like Bitcoin) into her crypto wallet, she had accidentally clicked on a scam link and had her wallet drained. After getting over her initial shock and embarrassment, Randi realized that not only was there a massive potential for blockchain technology to better the lives of artists, but there was also a huge opportunity to make it easier for others to understand and navigate the space.

"I never set out to be a thought leader in the Web3 space," Randi tells me. "I just thought that if I was putting all of this energy and effort into learning about NFTs and crypto, I might as well create easily digestible videos so other people could learn alongside me." Before long, Randi started getting invited to speak on panels at various NFT conferences and was even asked to advise other founders in the Web3 space.

"So many of us spend our entire lives trying to play catch up in industries that already exist," Randi says. "But if you are willing to be a little vulnerable, there is a lot of opportunity to quickly establish yourself as an expert on the ground floor of something new." Yet, becoming an armchair expert wasn't quite enough for Randi. Eventually, she decided it was time to found another company of her own, this time with a complete stranger she had met over the Internet in a Discord server – yours truly.

Over the past two years, Randi and I have been on a journey of navigating the ups and downs of the crypto industry as start-up founders. We have seen both companies and individuals come and go, a phenomenon that Randi is no stranger to from her early Web2 days. "No one knew if Web2 as we know it today was going to catch on . . . it just wasn't user-friendly enough," Randi says. "Then there were the people who worked hundred-hour weeks and got burned out emotionally and physically, leaving Facebook or the entire tech industry entirely before things really started to take off."

While Randi still believes the technology has some catching up to do in Web3, she has high conviction in and has already seen this new version of the Internet unlock new opportunities and connections for creators she had never thought possible. "I never even gave a minute's thought to becoming an art collector," Randi says. "I always thought you either had to have close relationships with galleries or had to be really knowledgeable about art." Yet, through the community we have built with HUG, Randi now has relationships with artists from all around the world, owning their work not just onchain in her wallet but as physical items including a custom-designed marathon jersey she has worn across her several races.

Today, Randi continues to balance her passion for entrepreneurship alongside her love for art and emerging tech, as well as a newfound love for running – a casual hobby she once had in her 20s but had given up on since having three kids. "So much of what I have done in my life has always been attributed to me being Mark's sister or so-and-so's business partner, or being Brent's wife, or even being my children's mother," Randi says. "When I cross the finish line in a race, however, no one can say that it's because of anything or anyone else other than me and my own hard work." For the first time and at age 42, Randi is finally feeling like the main character in her life, both in real life and on the Internet.

As we continue into the rest of this book, I hope that Randi's story, together with several other digital mavericks, will show you that there is no one way to navigate this rapidly evolving Web3 space. Not only that, but as overwhelming as all of this new technology is, it is never too late, nor could you ever be too old to be a beginner. As Randi tells me often, "Once you are forced to show up and suck at something, you realize it's really not that bad."

Let us continue.

2

Taking Back Control

IN THE YEAR 2020, the world was confronted with a reality it was not prepared to face – the COVID-19 pandemic. Today, we are still grappling with its aftermath, be it the loss of life, debates around vaccine side effects, our attitude toward remote versus in-person work and learning, and much more we have yet to wrap our heads around.

Even among my group of friends, the "pandemic years" affected all of us in dramatically different ways. Some of us mourned the loss of loved ones, jobs, businesses. Others thrived, discovering a new sense of purpose from interests and hobbies that ended up having more permanence than a temporary obsession with sourdough starter. For me, the pandemic reminded me of a dream that I had been holding on to for over 10 years, that is to move to and live in the city of Los Angeles.

My love affair with LA aside, the pandemic was likewise a time of introspection and reckoning for most. Suddenly affronted with long periods of solitude, many turned to the Internet to get inspired, educated, and entertained. Amid viral TikTok dances (which I was absolutely awful at), waves were being made across yet another Web2 social app – Clubhouse.

Clubhouse is a social audio app that was founded in the fall of 2019. With most social media platforms being text- (Twitter) or image-heavy (Instagram), Clubhouse felt unique and different. Users would join "rooms" to listen to or participate in live audio conversations, and the ability to interact with real human voices in real time felt like a departure from the otherwise performative nature of social media most of us were used to. Cue the pandemic, and the invite-only Clubhouse started to experience surging popularity as the sound of voices from complete Internet strangers and celebrities such as comedian Kevin Hart and TV personality Oprah Winfrey became a much-needed antidote to the void and loneliness we were all experiencing from being socially distant.

Clubhouse quickly became home to conversations across several topics ranging from sports to mental health, but the most popular by far were around that of start-ups and emerging technology. While blockchain technology wasn't new (Bitcoin had been founded a good decade earlier), it was still a relatively niche topic of interest, and for the first time, Clubhouse provided a place for discussions to start coalescing around both what the blockchain was and what it could do. In a time that challenged everything we knew about how to lead our lives, it felt natural for us to be open to new technology to reimagine not just the way we communicated but also how we consumed information as well as transacted with each other. Simply put, COVID-19 presented an opportunity to fast-forward both conversations about and the adoption of technology in many industries that were suffering from nationwide lockdowns. Art was one of them, and NFTs as an implementation of blockchain technology was proving a potentially viable solution for artists to monetize their work even without the ability to sell in physical galleries or art shows.

Many artists that are considered pioneers in the NFT space were not new to creating. Indeed, years later, amid the boom and bust of NFT hype cycles, I often have to remind people that artists didn't wake up one day proclaiming themselves as such because of NFTs. Instead, NFTs were merely an additional way for them to monetize their artwork, and in many cases expand upon their own creative practice.

In fact, many artists will resonate with the origin story of renowned animator DeeKay Kwon. DeeKay shared to X in August of 2023,

> You see, I used to believe that I was dumb, as I struggled to focus on any subject. My days were spent daydreaming and doodling, finding solace in my own art. I did dumb things here and there yada yada then I ended up going for art school later because drawing was [the] only skill I had. I took my first animation class and found myself immersed in drawing frame by frame for straight 8 hours, amazed by my newfound ability to focus which I never thought that I was capable of. I realized I am not dumb after all.
>
> Sadly, I didn't get to graduate. The 2007 financial crisis led to my parents' business collapsing, [so] I had to step in to help. But I won't bore you with my money struggle stories; everyone has their own. I ended up okay! [A] few years later, I was hired at a production company. They said they'll pay me 50 bucks a day for sitting in front of a computer doing animation. I thought I was gonna be rich!
>
> Ten years passed, I leveled up my animation skills, freelanced for major companies like Google and Apple, and eventually settled into a steady job at Apple. Financially stable but there was a creative void. So, I spent [the] rest of my day after work creating my own art that I am truly passionate [about]. Then, I'd share that on Instagram for 7 years. Positive feedback from my growing audience, which reached 400k followers, fueled my motivation. There was zero money for doing so, but that's okay because likes and comments were everything for me to keep creating. Life is good.
>
> Then boom! NFTs. You know the rest of the story. Fortunes came my way, freeing me from the corporate grind. I embraced a nomadic work lifestyle, supporting my family and enjoying newfound

financial freedom. The days of fretting over an $18 lunch is no more. Never imagined my life would be like this ever and it's still surreal to me. Life was good back then but it's even better now.

You see, even if everything goes to shit and I am forced to go back to the corporate world, I'd be okay. I'd still create art for those likes and comments. That's what truly fulfills me – connecting with all of you through my art. Without it, I legit don't know what I'd do with my life.

There is so much to process in DeeKay's story, but what stuck out to me was this. For years, he had lived his life doing what he loved – connecting with people through his art. Yet, it wasn't till NFTs that he was able to make a living and find financial freedom by doing so. More recently, DeeKay's work *Hands of Time* achieved a landmark sale of $200,000 at a Christie's auction.

Not every creator will achieve the same success as DeeKay. In a report published by Arts Council England in 2018, just one third of the money earned by visual artists come from their art, and nearly 70% of them have to take on additional jobs to make ends meet. A similar report by BFAMFAPhD, a collective formed in 2012 to advocate for cultural equity in the United States, found that just 10% of art school graduates are able to make and sustain a living from their artwork, a number that is likely far less for artists who are not formally trained. What's worse, none of these numbers account for the racial and gender disparity that clearly still exists in the art world today.

So while NFTs aren't the be-all and end-all, what they bring to the table in terms of provenance,[1] i.e. a proof and record of ownership, provides creators with another avenue to make a living for themselves. Instead of sharing their work on the Internet for nothing in return, digital creators now have the option of minting their work to the blockchain, which (a) establishes permanence and proof that their work originated from them, and (b) gives them the option of selling and monetizing their digital creations.

From the perspective of the end consumer, they also now have the opportunity to demonstrate themselves as a "true fan" for the creator. A true fan as defined by Kevin Kelly's breakthrough essay, "1000 True Fans," is one that will buy anything their favorite creator produces. For someone like myself who has always been inspired and enamored by the arts but was never given the blessing of my parents to pursue my interest in it, NFTs have allowed me to build one-of-a-kind connections with creators that truly make my world brighter and richer.

But wait, why do I speak about NFTs as if they are such magical things? Aren't they just silly monkey jpegs? Worse still, aren't they just a bunch of baloney?

> *New tech, old scams: Don't fall for these crypto and NFT ripoffs*
> *— CBS, March 2022*

> *NFT Scams, toxic "mines," and lost savings*
> *— The Guardian, May 2022*

> *The future vision of NFTs are looking far more banal*
> *— ArtNet, December 2022*

These are just a handful of the sensationalist headlines that we've seen in the press. It is no surprise that the casual viewer has got the "ick" by NFTs and anything and everything that is associated with it.

The issue here, however, isn't with NFTs; it has to do with basic human instincts that fear what we don't understand. To put things into perspective, here are a couple of headlines that emerged about the Internet from over 20 years ago. What seems ludicrous now was simply a natural knee-jerk reaction to the unknown, and that very same reaction is exactly how most people feel about NFTs today (Figure 2.1).

But you don't have to be most people. If we can just suspend our fear and disbelief for a moment and be open to understanding

Figure 2.1 "Internet 'may be just a passing fad'" from the *Daily Mail*, December 2000.

Source: Fresh On The Net/Flickr

what NFTs truly are – and by that, I mean the technology – you will soon start to realize that NFTs are no more of an avenue for scams than SMS or email. They are simply a vessel for information, but one more powerful than anything we've seen yet.

By opening ourselves up to understanding, we too are taking back control, just like DeeKay, just like the thousands of creators who have turned to NFTs to stretch the limit of what they can do and earn from their work. At the end of the day, the choice is yours – you can either fight technology or accept it and, moreover, fear its consequences or control them.

***

> **MEET A MAVERICK:** How Foodmasku Is Changing the Face of Visual Art One Food Item at a Time
>
> Foodmasku (aka Antonius Wiriadjaja) is a multimedia artist best known for turning meals into face masks before eating them. He has been recognized by the *New York Times* as one of Five Instagram Art Accounts to Follow, and has had his work showcased globally at events such as the TED Conference and the United Nations SDG Summit. Apart from being a renowned crypto artist, Antonius also teaches in the Art and Design department of Queens College, New York, and is an advocate for gun violence prevention after surviving a shooting near his Brooklyn apartment in 2013.

From crocheting to baking, many of us found ourselves picking up or revisiting an unexpected hobby during the pandemic. For me, because I was deeply manifesting (i.e. attempting to turn thought into reality) a move to LA, this ended up becoming a fascination with crystals and what kind of energy different rocks and minerals could introduce to my life. As absurd as that sounds, it fails in comparison to Antonius Oki Wiriadjaja's accidentally newfound craft of making face masks out of food . . . so much so that he now goes by the name Foodmasku.

Antonius was an artist long before food masks became his thing. Born in Jakarta, Indonesia, Antonius immigrated to the United States at age eight together with his parents and four siblings. Ethnically Chinese, the Wiriadjaja family felt compelled to leave Indonesia during a discriminatory period in the country's history known as the New Order despite having roots there dating back over 900 years. Like other Chinese Indonesians during the time, they were treated as second-class citizens and were forced to turn their backs on their heritage. In fact, when Antonius returned to Indonesia as a Fulbright Scholar over 20 years later, he was surprised to find out that the celebration of Chinese

New Year, which was previously banned in his childhood years, had since been legalized.

Being the youngest, Antonius assimilated to US culture the easiest out of his family, picking up English and quickly becoming the self-appointed family interpreter. Even though he recalls himself being really good at math, Antonius identifies more so as being a "very strange and creative child." Sure enough, it ended up being the left side of Antonius's brain that paved the way for college. Even though he ended up majoring in cognitive science, it was a creative scholarship that took Antonius to Hampshire College in Amherst, Massachusetts.

Prior to college, Antonius was exposed to different art forms through his internship at the Museum of Fine Arts slide library in Boston. "I feel so old saying this, but back then, you couldn't just go onto the Internet and find information about an artist or artwork," Antonius recalls. "People would come in asking to look for a certain piece by a particular artist . . . I would look it up on their behalf, and learn all about art history in the process." Antonius's exposure to art went beyond what was found in books, as he also got the opportunity to document new art installations by renowned artists such as Takashi Murakami, a Japanese contemporary artist known for his collaborations with the likes of Louis Vuitton and Kanye West.

Despite pursuing what would be considered a more pragmatic major in college (no doubt under the pressure of Asian parents, which I relate to wholeheartedly), it was clear that Antonius's creativity was irrepressible . . . although not necessarily in a well-received way. "Every single time I did something creative like writing or making a piece of art, it really offended somebody," he says. "Once, I made a digital artwork that made it to the cover of a school publication. People got really upset because digital art wasn't as widely accepted as other traditional mediums like oil painting and watercolor at the time."

It was receiving criticism at this early age that made Antonius question whether he had what it took to be an artist. "I wasn't sure if I had the mental fortitude or thick enough skin to be an artist," he says. One thing led to another, and Antonius ended up taking on a research assistant role at the Veterans Hospital in Boston as his first job out of college.

But it didn't take long for him to answer his creative calling. While Antonius was conducting MRIs by day, his performances at night were of a different nature. He joined the Theater Offensive, a drag group that included well-known members such as Katya of RuPaul Drag Race fame, to put on guerrilla performances around Boston to promote education around safe sex.

Within a couple of years, Antonius could no longer envision himself on the career path that he was on, especially since it involved years of postgraduate studies to become a clinical psychologist. Instead, Antonius craved a move to New York City – a city that he had already been escaping to every Sunday instead of going to church after his priest had made disparaging comments against homosexuality. This experience, coupled with his advocacy work with the Theater Offensive, reflected Antonius's deep sense of social justice, whether or not he was aware of it at the time.

Antonius took a leap of faith, quitting his job, withdrawing his 401(k) to establish a new life in New York. Easier said than done, this involved taking a variety of odd jobs from being a catering waiter to making uninspiring animated gifs for PR agencies. Eventually, just as how Antonius found the Theater Offensive in Boston, he found his home away from home in New York – the Interactive Telecommunications Program (ITP) at New York University (NYU)'s Tisch School of the Arts.

Founded by Professor Red Burns with the purpose of developing and harnessing creative technology, it was here that Antonius learned everything from coding to soldering his own circuits. Together with new video, animation, and audio tools, Antonius eventually expanded his repertoire to new media artwork, including what is perhaps his most spectacular work, "The Pool" – a large-scale animated exhibition of swimmers in a pool that was displayed in the lobby of the IAC Building, which is considered one of American architect and designer Frank Gehry's masterpieces.

Antonius had never dreamed of becoming a full-time artist. He recalls, "I always thought that I would be doing something else and doing my art on the side. I just didn't think it could be a viable profession." Yet, his very own accomplishments were starting to prove this sentiment wrong.

All of this came to a screeching halt on July 5, 2013. It was a hot summer day like any other, until Antonius got caught in the crossfire of a drive-by shooting as he was walking to a subway station in Brooklyn. He was shot once in the chest, with the bullet narrowly missing his heart and traveling to his stomach instead. Antonius was rushed to the hospital and placed under a sedated coma. Waking up from it a week later, he recalls, "I remember being the happiest I had ever felt in my life, but also the angriest. The only thing I knew how to do was make art."

And make art he did. Antonius took pictures of his scars every single day, from the day he was discharged from the hospital until his shooter was arrested and put on trial. The series of photos went viral, became a part of anti-gun violence campaigns, and thrust Antonius in the national spotlight.

While advocating an end to gun violence remains a core part of Antonius's identity and purpose in life, his photo series also prompted a deeper exploration of analog work after years of working on new media creations.

This and his experience with social media virality prepared him well for what was to come in April 2020. A month into lockdown, Antonius was having a Zoom meeting to figure out what he was going to do with a series of art exhibitions, now that they were clearly not going to go ahead as planned. One of his colleagues showed up to the meeting with an augmented reality (AR) filter in the form of a pickle – embarrassed – as she was unable to navigate to the right buttons to turn it off.

Without missing a beat, Antonius grabbed a piece of kale off his dinner plate. Using the materials he had bought to make his own fabric face masks due to the citywide shortage of N95s, Antonius made his first food mask and proclaimed, "Look, I have a filter on too!" Everyone on the call burst out laughing. It was the first time any of them had heard laughter in a month.

Antonius's first face mask led to a series of dares from his collaborators. "Somebody said, 'I bet you can't put on a lasagna,'" Antonius says. "I ended up making a lasagna from scratch and made a mask out of it." Before long, Antonius was making masks out of different foods everyday – anything from challah bread to instant pot noodles, taking self-portraits, and uploading them to Instagram.

Again, Antonius experienced overnight virality, with one of his videos garnering over 3.6 million views. In a few months, the *New York Times* included his account as one of the Five Instagram Art Accounts to Follow. Along the way, he co-opted the name Foodmasku, which was coined by his Indonesian partner as a form of endearment. Mas - ku means "my brother," "my friend," or "my lover" in Bahasa Indonesia and Javanese, depending on the context.

After the gun-shooting incident, Antonius (now Foodmasku) was only too familiar with the double-edged sword that social media virality is. "The pros are obviously that many people see and recognize your work," he says. "The cons are, the majority of them will inherently not understand it and take it out of context. These people will say some really hurtful things, not realizing that you, the artist, are going to read them."

With his food masks, however, Antonius was not prepared for others stealing his content. "At the time, people were taking my Instagram content and posting them on TikTok without my permission. I wasn't even on TikTok at the time and had to make an account just to get the content taken down, which in itself takes over a week," Antonius says. "That first week is when the person that posted gets all the benefits, all the views, and all the money that's associated with the content . . . none of which goes to the original creator. I was pretty mad, not only because I never got anything out of these videos but because other people who came across the content were also taking them out of context."

Frustration over the lack of control or ownership he had of his own content was what led Antonius to discovering NFTs. "I literally googled how to own a digital video, and that's how I found out about NFTs," Antonius says. Soon after, he found out that a couple of his friends, film directors Pamela Reed and Matthew Rader, had been selling their work on an art NFT marketplace known as Foundation, which at the time was still invite-only.

Antonius received an invitation to Foundation from Pamela and Matthew and within a day, sold his viral video as an NFT, and the money he made was enough to pay his rent for the month. "I remember thinking, I bet this is a fluke. But since I had all this magic Internet money and didn't really know what to do with it, I decided to put the money into minting additional artwork. It's crazy to think now, but back then, minting an NFT really did cost hundreds of dollars." That investment paid off. In 2021, Antonius ended up making a healthy six-figure income from selling hundreds of his artworks.

While being able to monetize his craft was undoubtedly enticing, provenance on the blockchain was what made Antonius a full believer in the power of NFTs. "I didn't really get NFTs at first until I realized that it could show that I was the original creator of my art," Antonius says. "At one point, there was a big brand that wanted to make food masks similar to what I had created. I was able to point to the ledger on the blockchain to show the date that my work was minted, and it was really cool to be able to refer to that as pseudo evidence, even if it didn't end up actually going to the court of law."

"When NFTs were first presented to me, it was more about how artists can finally make a living out of their work," Antonius says. "But to me, it's deeper than that. It's about transparency and ownership over who created what."

Coming up to the fourth anniversary of Antonius's very first food mask, it is perhaps befitting that he is now more widely known as Foodmasku. His art has been licensed by Meta to be part of nationwide campaigns for Facebook and Instagram, has been displayed on billboards all over the world, and has most recently taken him to the United Nations General Assembly to be a part of the conversation about global food waste. With or without the help of NFTs, there is no doubt his work has gained the recognition and the platform it deserves.

Today, aside from working on his art, Antonius is also passing on everything he has learned to the younger generation. Currently also an art and design professor at CUNY Queens College, Antonius not only teaches his students about what the blockchain is but also offers more practicable tips on how they can create their own smart contract in order to set up their own provenance. "My students who are between seventeen and twenty-two years old all view the blockchain as an inevitability," Antonius says.

"While they don't completely understand how it works, my students talk about how everything is going to involve Web3 in the future. In fact, some of them find it boring, because even something like the DMV will be on the blockchain eventually," Antonius laughs. Indeed, what Antonius said in jest has already started turning into reality. In August 2024, California announced the successful digitization of 42 million car titles on the Avalanche blockchain, even if moving the title transfer process onchain may still take a while.

Till then, I look forward to seeing Foodmasku's work go viral several more times . . . only this time, there will be no questioning who the original creator is behind it (Figure 2.2).

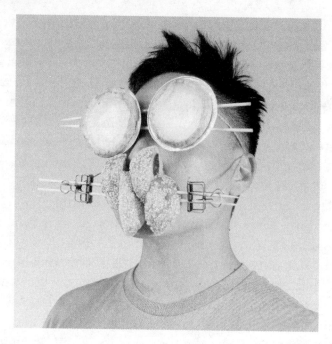

Figure 2.2 One of Foodmasku's artworks.
Source: With permission of Antonius Wiriadjaja.

3

Of Sliced Bread and Paper

IN 1928, THE Chillicothe Baking Company located in Chillicothe, Missouri, became the first company to pioneer sliced bread. Behind this was the Rohwedder Bread Slicer (invented by Iowa inventor Otto Rohwedder), which made uniformly sliced bread not just a reality, but eventually synonymous with any hyped up new product or invention.

Indeed, any truly groundbreaking innovation should become as commonplace and ubiquitous as sliced bread. In fact, the first record of the saying "the greatest thing since sliced bread" was made in reference to the television in 1952.

Well, before television and well before sliced bread, there was one other significantly overlooked revolutionary invention: paper.

Now, why are we going back in history, and what on earth has paper got to do with Web3 and NFTs? Well, paper is the perfect metaphor for them, and I thank my friend and X content creator Daniel Tenner (aka Swombat) for coming up with it. According to Daniel, "NFTs are like digital pieces of paper," and paper is "an incredibly powerful and versatile technology."

With that, we are going to break down all of the technical concepts you need to know using paper, and in doing so help define what some commonly used terms are and how they differ.

First Off, Paper Is Awesome

Indeed it is. Think of all the things you can do with paper. You can draw on it – and not just silly scribbles (though those are delightful in their own right); you can also draw diagrams to explain your concepts. These days with AI, you could even sketch out an entire wireframe and turn it into a website – a development that is lightly touched on in Part 3.

You can also write anything you want on paper! Maybe it's year-end holiday greetings. Maybe it's your inner Taylor Swift penning lyrics and musical notes. Or maybe it's drawing up agreements, contracts, laws, just like the United States Constitution (Figure 3.1).

Paper can also be used to represent money and wealth – from dollar bills to title deeds of your house and car. Even things such as passports, birth certificates, and school transcripts are recorded on paper.

Point is, you can do countless things with paper. And while it's hard to imagine a time before paper, there were less optimal mediums back then to communicate and record our thoughts and ideas – think cave walls, tree bark, clay tablets.

NFTs Are Just Magical Pieces of Digital Paper

Many years after paper was invented 2,000+ years ago, we have found ways to ensure that what is recorded on paper becomes more durable, primarily by digitizing it.

To further understand NFTs we will look at them as a continued evolution of how we digitize and store paper records. Let us take health records as an example. Back in the 80s, your health records were likely recorded on paper and categorized according to alphabetical order in a filing cabinet. When computers came along, these paper records then got stored digitally, but only on the local hard drive in the computer at your doctor's office. Should that hard drive get corrupted, your health records if not

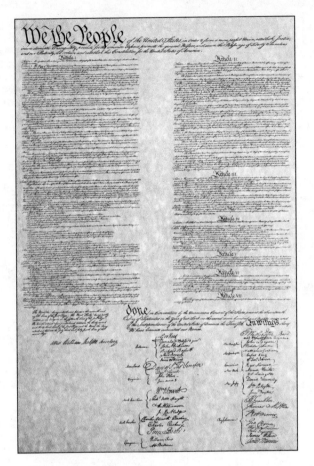

Figure 3.1 The United States Constitution.

Source: Jack/ Adobe Stock

backed up elsewhere, would immediately become lost and unrecoverable.

The advent of the Internet and cloud computing eventually allowed your digitized health records to be stored and made accessible online, making them less vulnerable to a single errant computer. While not immediately obvious, this is still a centralized way of storing your information. If the major servers hosting your information (think Google or Amazon Web Services) were to have some major outage, your health records could still get lost and become permanently irretrievable.

Even if server outages were to be avoided, your health records are still technically hosted and in some ways being held in custody by your medical provider – not you. Think about it – to switch medical providers, you will need to call and request for those records to be transferred, as opposed to being able to do it yourself.

Enter NFTs. Whoever came up with the term is clearly not a branding person, because prior to NFTs, I had barely ever heard the word non-fungible used in a regular sentence. That said, all non-fungible really means is that the item in question is unique and irreplaceable. Many things in life are non-fungible – from the house you live in to the journal entry you wrote as a 13-year-old.

Similarly, your health records are non-fungible, because they are uniquely yours and not replaceable or exchangeable with those of someone else's. This makes it possible for them to be digitized, stored, and recorded as a non-fungible token. And if they were, not only would your health records last forever, but they would also keep track of everything that has happened to or been recorded onto them. Further, if they were in your custody and ownership instead of your doctor's, you would also be able to move them freely as and when you wish.

As Daniel writes, NFTs are "like magic, somewhat intelligent, indestructible pieces of teleporting paper."

The Magic NFTs Run On Is the Blockchain

This "magic" that Daniel speaks of is the *blockchain* and is ultimately what forms the core of Web3. Okay, great, but what is the blockchain?

The blockchain is essentially a digital ledger of transactions that is not kept in one place (i.e. in a single hard drive or even a handful of offshore servers), but rather across an entire network of computers – making the storage of information decentralized.

Blockchain owes its name to how it stores all this transaction data, i.e. as blocks that are linked together to form a chain. Going back to the paper analogy, we can think of each block as a page, which is written on in order.

Each page (block) is then linked together using cryptography, which is a fancy way of saying code. Because of the code that links each page together, it then becomes not possible to go back and alter or delete prior pages.

In other words, after you have completed recording transactions on page 1, you have to go on to page 2, 3, and so on, and are unable to go back to page 1. In theory, this makes the blockchain tamperproof and is why people often refer to it as *immutable*.

Lastly, because a multitude of computers has signed off on the transaction occurring, not only is the record of the transaction secure, but it is also transparent and verifiable by everyone.

We Use Magic Money Called Cryptocurrencies to Operate on the Blockchain

Just like many things in life are non-fungible, we are also surrounded by a large number of fungible (read: replaceable, exchangeable) items. A dollar bill, for example, is fungible. That means if we are both holding on to a dollar bill, we would happily exchange it with each other, because its value is the same. The same applies to stocks or equity interest in a company.

Cryptocurrencies are fungible, and work in the same way as regular currencies, which are also referred to as fiat[1] currencies when issued by the government. And just like how different governments have different currencies, different blockchains (which are inherently different ecosystems) run on different cryptocurrencies. In the same way that I needed to convert my Singapore dollars into US dollars when I first moved to the US to pay for my rent and other living expenses, we too need to convert our fiat currencies into cryptocurrencies to transact on the blockchain. If we want to transact on the Ethereum blockchain for example, we would need to swap our US dollars (or whatever fiat currency we have) into Ethereum to do so. On the other hand, if we wanted to transact on the Solana blockchain, we would not be able to use Ethereum, and would need to get Solana instead.

Cryptocurrencies Can Be Used to Buy NFTs, Which Can Be Tied to Almost Anything

Going back to NFTs, if you are looking to purchase an NFT on the Ethereum blockchain, for example, you will then need Ethereum to complete the transaction. This transaction is then permanently recorded on the blockchain, making it authenticated and viewable to all. This also means that everyone will be able to see proof in ownership (when and how the NFT changed hands), and is also what people refer to as *provenance*.

Again, the NFT in question can be tied to almost anything. So when mainstream media refer to NFTs as silly monkey jpegs, that is only partially true. Monkey jpegs is an example of an asset that can be tied to an NFT, but so are things such as title deeds or health records. In fact, California's Department of Motor Vehicles (DMV), which is better known for nightmare lines, surprised everyone when they announced a partnership in 2023 to digitize car titles on the blockchain. This would allow drivers to hold car titles as NFTs and make it easier to streamline title transfers between owners.

Just like paper, an NFT has far more use cases, and is a "foundational, fundamental, incredibly versatile technology with near infinite use cases" (according to Daniel Tenner). To fear NFTs and cryptocurrencies would be like fearing paper. Do not fear paper. Do not shun the improvements it can bring to your life . . . do not shun sliced bread.

When I was nine years old and just finishing up third grade in elementary school in Singapore (otherwise known as being in Primary 3), I was tasked alongside everyone else to take a test to see if I qualified for the Gifted Education Program (GEP). Another unique (and at times criticized) part of the Singapore education system, this was a program aimed at identifying and meeting the needs of "intellectually gifted students."

The GEP program itself aside, the selection tests included questions not just on English and math, but also a series of questions aimed at testing one's spatial intelligence. Think . . . trying to figure out how a dice would come together based on what it looks like unfolded (Figure 3.2).

Now, I hated spatial intelligence questions. Heck – I can barely figure out directions without the help of GPS. If you are like me and find "visualizing with the mind's eye" challenging, you too may find the concept of NFTs as magical pieces of digital paper mind-boggling. Nonetheless, the more you see them being applied in everyday life, the more second nature they will become.

You see – NFTs can be anything digital, so much so that I am convinced that the term "NFT" will become redundant, just like how we stopped saying we listen to MP3s (we are just listening to music).

Even today, there are a number of digital assets that are cleverly hiding the fact that they are NFTs for fear of putting off the

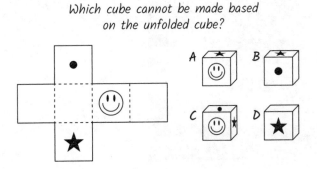

Figure 3.2 Example of a spatial intelligence test question.

general populace. Reddit Collectible Avatars are one such example. First launched by the popular social media platform in July 2022, nearly 25 million people today own their own version of the brand's alien mascot Snoo, decked out in outfits and accessories designed by independent creators. These avatars, which are used as profile pictures by Reddit users (also known as Redditors), are NFTs, but that is merely a footnote, not the highlight (Figure 3.3).

Similarly, Starbucks experimented with an extension of its Starbucks Rewards program through a beta program called Starbucks Odyssey. While Starbucks Odyssey has since been discontinued to "prepare for what comes next as we [Starbucks] continue to evolve the program," it was a prime demonstration of what onchain consumer loyalty could be. In Starbucks Odyssey, customers earned collectible stamps (which are – you guessed it – NFTs) by completing a variety of online games, quizzes, and

Figure 3.3   Collectible Avatars on sale on Reddit.

activities (such as buying coffee), which could then be exchanged for discounts and other types of unique coffee experiences. If this sounds no different from Starbucks' regular Rewards program, it's because it should not. While some may interpret the discontinuation of Starbucks Odyssey as a bearish signal for Web3, I see it more as a signal for Starbucks Rewards eventually going onchain (even if it may be a massive undertaking that would take years), instead of the company having to maintain two separate programs.

In short, NFTs aren't a unique product in themselves – they are just a new technology that is powering the things we already know and love today.

***

Now, if this is as far as you get into this book, you should be proud. By now, you should have some understanding of how the Internet has evolved (from Web1 to Web2 to Web3), what NFTs are, and a few insights into how they are currently being used and have made a difference to the lives of creators.

If this is where you want to stop, that's great. At the very least, you will be more discerning of media headlines, and be an informed observer of how this exciting and novel technology continues to evolve and develop.

But if you would like a front row seat to the Internet revolution we are currently in, if you would like to shape and not just witness change, it's time to sharpen your weapons, and read on.

> **MEET A MAVERICK: How Jesse Pollak Is Living Out His Beliefs by Being Based on Base**
>
> Jesse Pollak is the creator of Base and a VP of engineering at Coinbase, where he aims to bring a billion people onchain. Prior to Base, Jesse led Coinbase's consumer-facing engineering from early 2017 to mid-2021, including leading teams that worked on building Coinbase, Coinbase Pro, and Coinbase Wallet.

There's probably nothing that dates you more than finding yourself confounded by a slang that's all of a sudden widely used by a generation younger than the one you were born in. The word "based" is one such term. In an interview with *Complex* magazine that dates all the way back to 2010, rapper Lil B, who is widely credited with popularizing the term, describes *based* to mean "being yourself," "not being scared of what people think about you," and "not being afraid to do what you wanna do." On TikTok, the hashtag for the word has billions of views and is used by creators all over the world to label videos that relate to the idea of being original and unaffected by common culture.

By this very definition, Jesse Pollak is without a doubt, based. While many people stumble into leadership, Jesse's life on the other hand looked like a straight up assist for him to step up and lead a revolutionary movement. Born and raised in the Washington, DC, area, Jesse grew up playing competitive soccer, eventually captaining his high school soccer team. More important than his adolescent career as a center forward, however, was him attending a Quaker school, which instilled in him values of Quakerism throughout his childhood and teenage years.

Dating back to the mid-17th century in England, Quakerism was viewed as a countermovement to traditional Christianity as it rejected the complexity and hierarchy of the church at the time. Instead, it preached the equality of all persons, which remains a central tenet of the Quaker faith till today. While Jesse does not view himself as being particularly religious, it is clear that he still lives by Quaker values, which he is able to recite off by heart without pause – simplicity, peace, integrity, community, equality, and stewardship, otherwise known to its observers by the acronym SPICES.

"I did not grow up very religious, but I always identified with the values of Quakerism that I found to be very grounded in humility and a desire to make the community work more effectively together," Jesse says.

Indeed, while the importance of a mindfulness practice for most feels like something that has only emerged in the last few years, in part fueled by the pandemic, this is something that has been ingrained in Jesse from a young age. "Every week, we would come together for a Quaker meeting where everyone sits in a room silently for an hour and community members can rise to share what's on their mind and if they have been moved," Jesse recalls. "Getting to do that every week growing up introduced me to being present and having a mindfulness practice early on."

Quaker values were not just something that Jesse practiced behind closed doors. He recalls one summer after eighth grade when he and a handful of friends got into a sticky situation. The group of four hid some poorly rolled joints inside a cutout in the book, known to them as the "secret garden." When the book was discovered by one of his friends' moms, however, the two others in the friend group denied involvement. Jesse, on the other hand, decided to come clean, despite not being present when the discovery was made. To him, it was important to support his friend and also step up to ensure fair treatment. His confession ended up getting him grounded for the entire summer. "It felt like a really formative moment for me of showing up to do the right thing . . . and to back your friends and own whatever decisions you have made, even if they are bad ones," Jesse says. Till today, not only have Jesse and his best friend maintained their close relationship; their families now live next to each other despite having moved across the country to the Bay Area.

Jesse's move to the West Coast started farther south at Pomona College, a small liberal arts school in Southern California. Yet, having learned how to code in senior year of high school, Jesse already had a sense that a traditional college path may not be the right one for him. "I knew from the time I got to college that while I like the people and the community part of it, I did not actually like the 'schooling' part of it," Jesse tells me. "I've always been a very tactile learner, and found that I learned better by doing rather than by reading books."

Jesse's interest in computer science was also fueled by a well-known visionary that came before him. "I grew up watching Steve Jobs and all of his Apple keynotes, and would go away from those trying to jailbreak iPhones and learning what I could about them," Jesse recalls. "I think since then, I always had this idea of wanting to be someone who created products that millions and even billions of people could use."

Rather than wait till graduation to make that a reality, Jesse started building and shipping different applications in his first year of college. By the first summer, and after an internship at Buzzfeed in New York City, Jesse had cofounded a company called Clef, which focused on passwordless two-factor authentication. Eventually, Jesse decided to drop out of college early to move up to the Bay Area together with his two cofounders, Mark Hundall and B Byrne, and became a full-time founder.

Unfortunately, the Silicon Valley dream did not quite pan out as expected. "It was a really rewarding but also very challenging experience," Jesse says. "We never found product market fit, and we were pretty much grinding around the edges to make up for that sad reality . . . and that's pretty soul-crushing to do for five years."

Nonetheless, whatever product Jesse and his team had built was good enough to make them an acqui-hire target for both Twilio, a customer engagement app, and Coinbase, who was interested in the work they had done for crypto companies such as Bitfinex and BitMEX. Having already had a deep interest in cryptocurrency, Jesse accepted his portion of Coinbase's acqui-hire offer and joined as an engineer, parting ways with the rest of his team, who went on to join Twilio. At the time Jesse joined Coinbase, the company only had about 100 employees (as of the end of 2023, Coinbase employed over 3,400).

Jesse's introduction to cryptocurrency happened a good five years earlier, however, when he serendipitously found himself sitting across from someone by the name of Olaf Carlson in his college cafeteria. Carlson, who happened to be visiting a friend of Jesse's, was about to drive up the coast to start work at Coinbase – as its very first employee. Carlson later went on to be recognized in the *Forbes* 30 Under 30 list, and eventually became the founder and CEO of cryptocurrency fund Polychain Capital. Regardless, that very initial conversation was enough to get Jesse to start buying Bitcoin, reading its whitepaper written by Satoshi Nakamoto, and staying an avid observer of other historic crypto-related developments such as the crowd sale for Ethereum.

While Clef had served over 25 crypto clients, by joining Coinbase, Jesse finally took a front row seat in shaping the future of digital currencies and building the infrastructure required to "rewrite the world's financial systems." Over the next several years, Jesse worked on building up Coinbase, starting with a seven-person team to eventually managing hundreds of engineers. He led teams that worked on building and scaling products, including Coinbase, Coinbase Pro, and Coinbase Wallet across web, iOS, and Android. This also included an effort to rewrite the Coinbase apps from the ground up with React, a successful multiyear project that had a massive impact on the business.

Yet, as Jesse wrote in his 2017 Medium article when he first joined Coinbase, his primary motivation and interest in cryptocurrencies lay in its "opportunity to build new structures that increase economic opportunity and level the playing field." As fulfilling as it was to make Coinbase as user-friendly and accessible as possible, Jesse believed in doing more. Jesse started to ask himself, "What would it look like to bring Coinbase onchain? How do we start to catalyze that change even more inside the business?"

Together with a small team, Jesse took the lead on integrating, building, and supporting protocols at Coinbase, all of which have culminated in a new L2 blockchain, known as Base. As Jesse describes, "Base is a secure, low-cost, builder friendly Ethereum Layer 2 with the goal of bringing the next million developers and billion users onchain."[2]

From day one, Base was built as an open-source platform, meaning that anyone can build apps on it. "L2s are designed to help scale the blockchain, bundling transactions so they can be faster and cheaper. A transaction that can cost $10 on the L1 Ethereum network may cost only 1 cent on Base," Jesse explains. "Compared to Ethereum, you can take the same code for an app, run it, but have it cost up to 10,000 times cheaper, and as a result be more accessible to anyone around the world."

Base was officially launched on the Mainnet in August. Less than a year on, Jesse believes that Base is already establishing itself as a market leader for a number of reasons, but none more important than its community. "From an ecosystem and community perspective, the quality of builders on Base is basically unparalleled," Jesse says. "People are here to build high-quality products, and are here to put the team and product ahead of the individual. This is a really unique culture that I do not think is prevalent everywhere."

Indeed, this culture is present in the way Base rewards its builders through grant funding. "A lot of other protocols like to pay people to come and build with them," Jesse tells me. "We do not do that. We encourage people to come, build with us because they want to, and when these people deliver value, we are confident that they can get rewarded." To date, developers on Base have already earned over $50 million in retroactive grants from Base and Optimism,[3] resulting in what Jesse believes is a virtuous cycle that leads to an even bigger impact on the ecosystem over time.

Having been one of the earliest adopters of crypto, Jesse has seen it all. And while Jesse is unwavering in his commitment to mass onchain adoption, he acknowledges that there's still room to go, in the form of "lower fees, better wallets, better identity" to evolve the narrative from crypto as a primarily speculative asset to one that is more about an enabling technology.

Today, Jesse has found himself as a leader of the rallying cry: onchain is the new online. While he credits Jacob Horne, the founder of Zora, an onchain media app and protocol, for coming up with the line, Jesse has no issue taking credit for popularizing and leading the charge behind it. "I've seen my words be able to serve as inspiration for a lot of people on their journey, and I hope that I'm able to continue doing that," Jesse says. "Obviously, there's pressure, and a lot of focus and attention, but if I'm just authentically myself and share how I see and view the world, people who share my beliefs will be naturally drawn to that. These are the people I'm excited to build with and build for."

While the mission to bring a billion people onchain as a way to "increase innovation, creativity, and freedom" is one that resonates on a global and history-defining scale, Jesse's advocacy for a better future is also very much focused on his local community. "Besides my friends and family, I'd say that the biggest thing I spend my time on is figuring out how to bring a more abundant mindset to the United States, and in particular California and the broader East Bay," Jesse says as a fifth-generation resident in the Oakland and Berkeley area. "I spend a lot of time and energy on social issues like how we increase housing, how we can have safer streets for pedestrians and cyclists, and just in general, how to support people to live better lives in our cities."

In speaking with Jesse, I am reminded of the first time I heard him speak on a panel in May 2023 at VeeCon, a conference put on by American businessman and Internet personality Gary Vaynerchuk. At the time, the market was undoubtedly bearish. Yet, instead of focusing on what many were terming a crypto winter, Jesse was rallying the crowd around the idea of a builders' spring. And in keeping to the same analogy of seasons, this ended up culminating in a campaign known as Onchain Summer when Base launched to the public a few months later.

While one would think that the increasingly positive market sentiment entering 2024 is validation of Jesse's optimism, he had a surprisingly different take. "There's actually a part of me that's like 'no – stop' to the market being positive again," Jesse laughs. "It's so much more distracting when there's all this noise and chaos. I just want to build because we still have so much work to do to bring billions of people onchain."

And that is exactly what it means to be *based*.

PART 2

How to Become a Maverick

It is impossible to be a maverick or a true original if you're too well behaved and don't want to break the rules. You have to think outside the box.

– Arnold Schwarzenegger

4

Step 1: Identify Your Glow Stick Moment

WHEN I WAS approached to write this book in the spring of 2023, I took pause. A long one. After all, I had only been working full-time in the world of Web3 and NFTs for a little under 18 months, and in my mind, I was probably closer to a fraud than an expert.

Then I remembered – almost no one is an expert in Web3, much less NFTs. Not yet anyway. Sure, Bitcoin was invented in 2009, and the first NFT was created 10 years ago in 2014, but most of the "esteemed" thought leaders you come across on X probably entered this space during the COVID years of 2021–2022. Not only that – all of us are still learning about the extent of what this technology can do, and are continually evolving and adapting our thinking given the volatility of markets and regulatory developments.

And for better or for worse, much of the commentary around anything crypto-related is linked to price speculation. Sure, the technology is incredibly powerful, but the use cases while proven, are still far from being widely adopted. This means that when the market experiences a downturn as it has done through 2022 and

2023, creators leave, companies downsize, and euphoria turns very much into despair.

Why then would anyone want to be a part of this emotional and financial roller coaster?

Because with the right precautions in place, roller coasters are a fun, thrilling, and at the end of the day, safe experience. Being an active participant in Web3 is very much the same.

Where does one start? After all, there are countless roles one can play in Web3. Heck, before we go into that, within Web3 itself, there are many communities and subcultures formed around different interests such as decentralized finance (DeFi), gaming, memecoins,[1] and art. If you are looking to truly immerse yourself and find your place in this ecosystem, you will first have to find the area that really speaks to and excites you.

NFTs, particularly on the art side, were mine. While my traditional conservative Asian upbringing discouraged me from actively considering a career in the arts, I had a deep admiration for the power of creative expression. After all, from performing in the choir and being part of an a cappella group to writing poems and making collage art, I spent years nurturing my creative side, even if it manifested only in hobbies and extracurriculars (Figure 4.1).

Needless to say, once I started wrapping my head around the basic concepts of Web3 and blockchain technology, I was most blown away by the digital art movement I was seeing unfold through NFTs.

I have spent my entire adulthood living in either a studio or one-bedroom apartment, which all had limited wall space. Art collecting also seemed like something that was completely out of reach and a pastime reserved for the elite. NFTs demonstrated the possibilities of being able to build a digital art collection of my own, to showcase not only my taste, but also my patronage for artists I looked up to and whose skills I deeply admired.

And while art may seem like one very limited use case for NFTs, it was my "glow stick moment" – the moment where you snap a glow stick, and can no longer undo or bottle the light that you have just created. And sure, as you start to uncover some of the challenges Web3 still has to overcome, that light may fade – but what's more important is that you cannot unsee its potential.

So start your maverick journey by identifying your glow stick moment – reflect on your existing interests or pain points, and learn how Web3 and blockchain technology can enhance or resolve them. Here are a few examples.

Say you are an avid gamer; you may very well find promise in the world of Web3 gaming, where players can actually own, trade, and sell in-game assets. Even though I am embarrassed to share that I am only an occasional gamer today (considering my

Figure 4.1 Collage art I made from magazines as a teenager.

Figure 4.1 (Continued)

preteen years of playing Neopets as well as Pokemon on a bootleg Gameboy emulator on PC), there is plenty to get excited about crypto gaming today.

One game that I am determined to participate in is called *Crypto: The Game*, which is inspired by the reality TV series *Survivor* – a show that I as a reality TV junkie am still watching today even into its 46th season. In *Crypto: The Game*, NFTs act as a player's entry ticket into the game. Just like *Survivor*, contestants are divided into tribes to compete in immunity challenges that take the form of arcade-style minigames, before having to vote each other out till one player remains as sole survivor. The onchain element here is fascinating as after a player is voted out, their NFT, which was previously earmarked as an entry ticket or player token, then evolves into a "jury voting token," which allows anyone holding on to one to vote for the eventual winner. Since NFTs are owned by the players, these can be sold at any point to allow others to take over their participation through the season. Already lauded to be "game theory on steroids," I cannot wait to see how following seasons continue to evolve especially as more onchain elements get incorporated.

If gaming is not your thing, you may find yourself fascinated by more everyday consumer applications, such as Starbucks' experimentation with its rewards program on the blockchain or how Ticketmaster is allowing concertgoers to unlock exclusive experiences through NFTs. In the latter, the ticketing platform teamed up with popular metal band Avenged Sevenfold in 2023 to provide holders of the band's *Deathbats Club* NFT collection early access to buy tickets. This is known as token-gating, where token holders can access exclusive benefits, which aside from early access can even extend to additional perks such as discounts or exclusive experiences.

In fact, Ticketmaster could probably have done with a much broader and earlier implementation of token-gated experiences to avoid the well-documented debacle that ensued around the sale of tickets to Taylor Swift's record-breaking Eras tour. While Ticketmaster attempted to allocate presale slots to "verified Swifties," the site ended up crashing when it was overrun with resale bots. Tickets sold out in seconds and were immediately available on ticket resale sites with markups as high as $30,000, priced out of reach for several diehard Taylor Swift fans. There are many ways that the use of NFTs and blockchain technology could have mitigated this. For example, tickets as NFTs could be made "soulbound" – soulbound NFTs are non-transferable, which prevents them from being sold and hence rendering them useless to scalpers.[2] Alternatively, imagine if NFTs were used to contain information about a fan's interaction with and hence fandom of Taylor Swift, from attending her prior shows to buying merchandise.

Token-gating would then allow her most loyal fans to rightfully gain preferential access to ticket sales of future shows.

While it will take a long time to overhaul the underlying technology of a behemoth such as Ticketmaster, and perhaps even longer to disrupt existing consumer behavior, thinking about how the blockchain can solve problems you encounter on a day-to-day basis can be incredibly illuminating for your glow stick moment – pun very much intended.

One last example I will provide is that of the world of DeFi (also known as decentralized finance), which is an umbrella term for a variety of financial applications on the blockchain geared toward disrupting financial intermediaries. At the intersection of NFTs and DeFi is what we call NFT finance, or NFTFi, which has a few different applications. One such example is the use of NFTs as collateral to borrow against. Similar to how someone takes a mortgage loan against their house as collateral, this would give the owner of the NFT additional financial utility.

All of this is still incredibly nascent and hence risky. However, if you have an interest in investing and having a diversified portfolio of products with different yields, you may find this the most fascinating application of them all! For better or for worse, and given both my consumer background and creative side, DeFi has become the part of Web3 that I have found the least amount of interest in. The most important thing to note is that's okay.

At the end of the day, Web3 is simply an all-encompassing term for a new Internet paradigm. Just like how we are unable to keep up with every single TikTok trend or every single piece of news that breaks on the Internet, we similarly will not be able to do it all in Web3. Hence, to really play a part in it, you need to first of all understand and know where you want to play. Grab your glow stick, and break it.

How to Identify Your Glow Stick Moment

I have written this book so that it will not just be made up of theories, but rather will provide actionable steps for everyone to take on their maverick journey. As such, each chapter in this section will be accompanied by a series of exercises or writing prompts to assist you in making the most out of what has been discussed.

To identify your glow stick moment, try to jot down answers to any or all of the following questions.

- What are some of your favorite pastimes both today and growing up?
- When was the last time something got you really excited? What was it and why?
- Who inspires you? What about their story and journey resonates with you?
- What are some of the everyday problems you encounter as a consumer of the Internet?

What industry do you currently work in or have you worked in the past? Do you see blockchain technology playing a role, and if so, how?

***

> **MEET A MAVERICK:** How Latashá Is Lending Her Voice to Inspire a New Generation of Independent Creators
>
> Latashá Alcindor, otherwise known as Latashá, is a multi-hyphenated entrepreneurial artist who creates communal experiences based on her stories of self-empowerment, autonomy, and healing. Initially known as an independent hip hop artist, Latashá's artistic range now extends to encompass dance, punk, and various other expressive forms. Latashá was previously head of community of Zora, a Web3 protocol and marketplace, and is now leveraging cutting-edge technologies such as blockchain and AI to redefine the future of creativity and community building.

The first time I saw Latashá perform was in March 2022 at a launch party for Female Quotient – an events and advisory company whose mission is to close the gender gap in the workplace. Female Quotient was celebrating bringing its signature Equality Lounge programming into the metaverse,[3] and there could be no better person to headline their event than Latashá. Latashá was dressed head to toe in a two-piece ensemble made out of pink silk, and looked as if she belonged on the set of the *Barbie* movie (a whole year and more before the movie was actually released). "Imma talk my shit," she rapped, before turning the microphone back to the crowd. "Imma talk my shit!" we roared back in unison.

You see, Latashá's unique ability to light up and command any room she's in is a palpable and undeniable energy. It's also something that has been a part of her for as long as she can remember. "I was so extra as a kid," Latashá recalls with a laugh. "Everyone tells me that I was always grabbing the karaoke microphone, singing and performing all the time."

Latashá was raised by a young mother and her stepdad in Flatbush, a neighborhood in Brooklyn, New York. While an only child, Latashá describes her childhood as being "surrounded by a Caribbean and Latina household that was pretty insane." Even then, Latashá found plenty of time to get lost in her own imagination. "I grew up imagining myself as an artist and a musician... I even put on little play concerts in my room while dressing up in my mom's clothes," Latashá says. It wasn't long before Latashá had to put pen to paper to find a big enough outlet for all of her irrepressible creativity and imagination.

Latasha's love for writing initially started off as innocent journal entries about teenage crushes. Yet, it wasn't till her teenage boyfriend passed away that she started using poetry as a way to heal and work through a lot of the deeper underlying emotions she had. Even then, it took years before she was able to really process and understand the feelings of grief she had chosen to suppress. "I was only 15 years old when my partner passed," Latashá says. "When he did, I honestly just blocked out my feelings because I was afraid of speaking and sharing about them. It wasn't till I was much older and started diving deeper into my music and my art that I was able to truly start healing."

A complete immersion into her art did not happen overnight for Latashá, even though it looked as if she was onto a promising start as a performance art and African American studies major at Wesleyan College. "As much as I hate the loans that I have from student debt, college was really the place that I was first able to identify as a creative," Latashá tells me. Indeed, it was through college that Latashá felt that she was finally able to explore and understand the various facets of her creative identity, and felt confident enough to start representing herself to the world as a spoken word artist.

Yet, to pay off her student loans and support her family, Latashá opted for more practical day jobs. She spent four years on and off working at the finance department of Chase Bank, while also juggling a handful of retail jobs at places such as Costco and Urban Outfitters. But while Latashá may have remained uninspired by day, she continued to inspire others by night. "At night, I would go and perform poetry slams at parties all around New York City," she says. "Before I knew it, people were starting to catch on to my spoken word and invited me to rap and perform with them."

Latashá, who did not even consider herself as a rapper at the time, shook off her disbelief and said yes to all of the opportunities that came her way. Before long, she was opening and sharing bills with some of the biggest hip hop artists in the world such as Q-Tip, Big Sean, and Kanye West. But as amazing as all of this was, Latashá could not help but feel that the music industry wasn't all it was cut out to be.

In fact, Latashá recalled harboring some of these misgivings even from her college days. "Studying African American studies shed a lot of light on how the system denigrates Black people, and beyond that, how poorly artists were treated . . . especially women." All of this proved to be true. "Not only did I have to deal with weird moments of harassment and unsolicited attention from men; I also had to deal with people trying to change my body and the way I looked," Latashá says.

Wrestling with both the opportunities and drawbacks that came with the music industry took its toll. All of a sudden, Latashá wasn't creating as much. "Mentally, I felt like I had to go about every single day being prepared for the worst, and worrying that the industry was just going to eat me up and chew me out," she says. "I'd say I kind of fell into a bit of a depressive state."

Eventually, Latashá decided she had to figure out what it meant to be an artist on her own terms. She went back to doing performance art for smaller shows in New York City, participated in residency programs at creative venues such as The Shed and National Sawdust, took odd jobs including making music for commercials, and most of all, was able to channel her creative energy into the one thing she loved best – writing.

Going independent did mean that Latashá's finances were more unstable and unpredictable, but to her, it was worth it. "People think that when you are an independent artist, it means that you do not have money and hence you aren't successful,"

Latashá says. "But what I learned from being independent is that success is up to each of us as individuals to define and determine for ourselves."

"For me, the most important part of my journey has been taking the time to get to understand and know myself," Latashá continues. "The most beautiful thing about being independent is that I have been able to make my own decisions and not have anything hold me back. Sure – making money may be hard, but I feel as free as I can be."

The freedom to work on her own projects was what connected Latashá with her partner, Jah. A filmmaker and visual artist himself, Jah ended up directing and shooting a bunch of Latashá's music videos, but perhaps more importantly, was the one who introduced her to the world of Web3 and NFTs a few years later.

Like many others, it was the pandemic, which resulted in both a failed publishing deal and a number of canceled projects, that turned both Latashá and Jah to the world of Web3. Latashá recalls the day that Jah told her he made his first NFT sale on an NFT marketplace known as Rarible. "I remember asking, what are you talking about? What's Rarible?" Latashá says. "I did not believe him initially, and told him he had to be careful. But soon enough, Jah started paying his bills, and I saw relief and excitement that I had not seen in him since the start of the pandemic."

Latashá quickly learned what she could about Web3 from Jah. By February 2021, she minted and sold her music video "Ilikedat" as an NFT, and became the first person to bring music videos as a medium and women's rap as a genre to the blockchain. "I'm not a huge fan of saying, oh – I'm the first, but it is still really cool to know that I ended up becoming my fullest creative self as part of a new world we were exploring."

Even then, Latashá is measured about how she onboards other creators to Web3. "At the beginning, Jah and I wanted to bring everyone we cared about and introduce them to NFTs," she says. "But as the market started to fluctuate, I took a pause, because I realized that not everyone is ready for what this space is and can do."

"In order to be successful in this space, you have to be able to deal with risk and be okay with losing sometimes," Latashá continues. "I've been a risk taker my whole life, and so I've learned to be okay with failures, and be okay with losing. This space may work for me, but it will not work for everybody because not everyone has the same kind of mindset."

The stakes are arguably higher for music artists. While visual art continues to make headlines and record-breaking sales on the blockchain, music NFTs continue to lag in both creator and collector adoption. "People just do not see the worth in music like they do for a visual piece. Music after all is not even something you can hold onto unless you have a music sheet," Latashá explains. "And today, we are valuing music at the lowest price we have ever had with the popularity of streaming platforms. So it's hard for people to grasp paying creators to own their music, and I totally understand that."

Latashá knows that ultimately the best way to encourage other artists to dip their toes into Web3 is through the power of stories, including her own. "I'm very grateful to be one of those people who can offer a new perspective on what Web3 can do," Latashá says. "But it's going to take new stories, new people at the forefront, and most of all, enough time to get it right."

Getting Web3 right requires platforms and creators to be in conversation with each other, and Latashá has made sure to play a role in facilitating that. After minting her first music video on the NFT marketplace Zora, she was invited by its founders Jacob Horne and Dee Goens to take on a more formal role in being a liaison with the company's growing community of independent Web3 creators. She became Zora's head of community before founding Zoratopia – a collective focused on accessible education and spotlighting diverse creators, which she has since rebranded to Topia. "The best part of my collaboration with Zora was having an opportunity to share with a large company what artists wanted, and putting artists' values at the forefront of the conversation,"

Latashá says. "I really do think it has benefited Zora in the long run, and it makes me so happy to see the platform continuing to blossom beautifully while caring deeply about artists."

Today, Latashá has stepped down from her role at Zora to focus her efforts on the next chapter of her career. "I've learned so much about the tools that I can utilize in Web3, and now I'm ready to use them to build a world for myself and my community to reside in and interact," Latashá shares. While her sound had been inspired early from hip hop stars such as Missy Elliot and Santigold, Latashá has more recently been working to expand her repertoire and influences to include electronic and dance. "This is something I've always wanted but was scared to do, because I did not know how my fans were going to react. But I've got myself to a point where I do not care what others think . . . in a loving way!" she adds.

As Latashá sits on the verge of revolutionizing her relationship with her fans both through her music and with the help of technology, she has a couple of pieces of advice for other creators trying to follow in her footsteps. "First, it's always about your art. Whenever you feel like a platform is overtaking the story, get back to the art, and get back to you."

Latashá's second piece of advice is that crypto is not the end all be all. Rather, it is part of a rich and ever-growing tool set she believes all creators should have access to in order to support their creative careers. "As you are evolving as a creative, use all the tools that you can, and let Web3 just be one of them." Latashá says.

While Latashá may have been spending the past year working on reintroducing herself and her music, one thing remains unchanged – it's always been about her telling her truth and talking her shit, with no one to tell her otherwise.

5

Step 2: Understand and Hold On to Your Why

AT THE END of 2013, I was less than two years into moving back to Singapore after college, and likewise less than two years into my first proper job, as an investment manager for Singapore's sovereign wealth fund. I was also a new dog mom, and a newly-wed, all before turning 25.

Plenty of "new" to soak in. And yet, it wasn't enough. Shortly after my 25th birthday in November, I decided I wanted to start my very own business. As a somewhat indentured servant to the Singapore government (they had paid for my college education in full, but I had to commit to working for them for six years in return), this business not only had to be a side hustle, but also one done on the down-low.

I took all of my life savings at the time and put them into my first start-up – Singapore's (and also Southeast Asia's!) very first indoor cycling studio – despite never having taken a SoulCycle class. Well, actually, I could barely cycle on a regular bike too, since being taught how to cycle somehow got omitted from my childhood amid grueling spatial intelligence tests.

Called 7Cycle, the studio resided in a three-story heritage shophouse located in the heart of Singapore's Central Business District. 7Cycle went on to become one of the best experiences I've had in my life, even though it ended my short-lived marriage in the process, and I ended up selling the business a couple of years after.

Because hindsight is always 20/20, I can now look back to my mid-20s and come to the realization that back then, I was simply chasing the next adrenaline-ridden project.

Even though I was responsible for managing hundreds of millions of dollars of taxpayers' money, somehow that wasn't stimulating or rewarding enough. Neither was raising a puppy (although I'm proud to report that that puppy is now aged 13 and is continuing to live out her golden years with me here in America) nor planning a wedding.

It took building a business from scratch (quite literally brick by brick) and then having to let it go for me to understand my why. That why is not just bringing people together, but also to help them see the extent of what they can accomplish in community with each other. As that well-known African proverb goes, "If you want to go fast, go alone. If you want to go far, go together."

After 7Cycle, it took me years to find something that embodied the same electrifying energy that came from within a dark room of over 30 sweaty bodies pedaling to the beat of music together. Surprise, surprise – that something is Web3.

While the Web3 community may be miles apart and be virtual Internet strangers, there was nonetheless an undeniable spirit of wanting to cocreate, and a willingness to learn and navigate this new paradigm together.

Today, through my company HUG, I have brought together over tens of thousands of artists from over 160 countries who connect with and inspire each other through their art daily. Hundreds of them also join us for live educational programming we put together to learn about new concepts such as dynamic NFTs[1] and incorporating AI into their creative process.

Not every Web3 community is like HUG however. And ours is by no means perfect either.

Thing is, while there are many in the Web3 and NFT ecosystem who are excited about meeting fellow mavericks and are similarly keen to learn about and experiment with various blockchains, platforms, and applications, there are also many who are here for different (and sometimes, even nefarious) reasons.

This is why Step 2 is about finding your why, and more importantly, being able to hold on to it, no matter what happens. Because we are still in the early innings of how the blockchain (and hence cryptocurrency) is going to be adopted, this space is ultimately still deeply speculative. This means that there's a lot of money to be made, and conversely, a lot of money that could be lost.

If you are interested in diving into Web3 purely for the money, that's fine. Recognize that to be your why and be cognizant of all the risks (both from scammers and market volatility) that are out there. Let this also be the point where I legally disclaim that *nothing I say, in this book or otherwise, is financial advice.*

But if money is not the only reason why you are here, this is a good time to really hone in on what those other reasons are.

Perhaps you are an artist who would like to explore a different way of monetizing your art and finding new collectors for your work. Or maybe you are interested in seeing how you can incorporate this technology into taking your creativity a step further, such as through dynamic NFTs.

Or maybe you are an avid collector who is interested in exploring the future of collectibility on the blockchain – that could be anything from art to sports to other forms of memorabilia.

Perhaps you are a brand guru, who would like to understand how concepts of digital ownership and community could affect how your brand is perceived and adopted by consumers of the future.

Or maybe you are a natural community builder and would like to apply those skills and foster meaningful connections without being limited by geography.

You may also be a developer, or a product person, who wants to delve into Web3 to either enhance your skills or bring unique insights to the table to make the existing experience easier to understand and more consumer-friendly (and boy, do we need it!).

Or maybe you are perfectly content with your day-to-day life and are simply here to learn and absorb as much as possible, while meeting some really cool people along the way.

Ultimately, there is no right or wrong why, but understanding what yours is when entering the Web3 space is critical. That's because if you surround yourself with folks with different whys from yours, your experience will more likely than not be an unpleasant, and potentially even unwelcoming one.

Lastly, more important than understanding your why is being able to cling on to it. While there are more people building behind the scenes than ever, the public court of opinion on X is naturally far more positive and excitable when prices are up than when prices are down. This can make you question why you are spending time and energy on all this Web3 stuff, because fact of the matter is, you are still early no matter how you feel or what others say.

Being a true maverick will require you to have the ability to tune out the noise, while also holding on to your personal reason for showing up and staying curious every single day.

> **How to Understand Your Why**
>
> Everybody's why is different. It is easy to jump into something just because our friends are doing it or because it seems the trendy thing to do at the time. Crypto and Web3 are no exception.
>
> In identifying your "why," it is important to apply the framework of the three whys, which is the practice of asking "why" three times to get to the real root of a question or problem.

The following questions are designed to help you dive deeper into your why, but for each one, you should keep asking yourself follow-up questions to drill in to what makes you tick.

- What you do on a day-to-day basis does not necessarily equate to what your why is. Is there something that you are passionate about that you could not bear to give up? How would you feel if you had to?
- If this were your last day in this world, what would you want to be remembered for? Have you already accomplished that?
- What made you pick up this book in the first place? What takeaways do you want to walk away with by the time you've completed it?
- At the risk of sounding like Marie Kondo, what sparks joy in you? Recall the last time you felt joyful. What happened then? Who was involved? How could you re-create that feeling?

Holding on to your why can often be harder than understanding it. Once you feel that you have understood your why, jot it down so you can be reminded of it. This could be as a pinned note in your Notes app, or on a Post-it that you can't miss. Every time things get a little shaky or uncertain, refer back to your why, and remind yourself what got you there in the first place.

***

> **MEET A MAVERICK: How Matt Medved and Alejandro Navia Are Changing the Way Stories Are Told through Stories of Their Own**
>
> Matt Medved and Alejandro Navia are cofounders of Now Media, a Web3-powered media conglomerate home to its flagship brand *nft now*, an award-winning digital media platform that serves industry-leading news and features about the Web3 and NFT community. Before Now Media, Matt founded Billboard Dance, and had also served as senior vice president of content at lifestyle publisher *Modern Luxury* and editor in chief of *Spin*, an American music and culture magazine. Alejandro has been an advisor, executive coach, and has also held leadership positions in media and AI at Verizon and Elite Daily.

On paper, there appears to be little in common between a history buff born and raised in Bogotá, Colombia, and a music aficionado hailing from Rochester, New York. Indeed, before they met, the lives of Alejandro Navia and Matt Medved could not have been more different. It would take a meeting of the minds years later to eventually prove none of that to matter when two people share a similar belief and vision for a better future.

Matt was born into a medical family with a neurologist for a father and a nurse for a mother. However, his upbringing was defined by something else entirely: music. "My father may not have a musical bone in his body, but he is probably the biggest Beatles fan I've ever met on earth," Matt says. "He collected all kinds of Beatles memorabilia, from all kinds of merchandise to signed vinyls, and more."

While Matt grew up fronting bands across a variety of genres, from punk to metal to pop, it was from songwriting that he uncovered the greatest depths of his creative expression. "I'm probably a better songwriter than singer," Matt laughs. Describing his high school band as the Doors meets Sonic Youth, Matt drew inspiration from the long poetic rants of Doors lead vocalist and lyricist Jim Morrison. "The lyrics he wrote resembled epics, so much so that the music itself became the soundtrack for the stories he was telling."

As Matt found himself inspired by the stories of music legends and penning ones of his own, Alejandro was over 1,000 miles away navigating an unexpected new chapter in his life. Alejandro, who was moved by his parents from Colombia to the US at age eight, described himself as quickly having to enter survival mode in what felt like an unfamiliar and at times, even hostile environment. "It was like a big rupture," Alejandro says. "One day, I'm taking my First Communion and two days later, I'm in South Florida and being told that was our new home."

Alejandro would go on to attend his first day of American elementary school just three weeks later, with only the most basic command of the English language. When first asked for his name in class, Alejandro responded proudly with his name in full: Luis Alejandro. To his confusion, his teacher shook her head and responded gently with, "No, you're just Luis." By leaving out his middle name, which was the name he was referred to his entire life by his family (to avoid confusion since he shared his first name Luis with his father), Alejandro recalls feeling unsafe for much of his formative years.

Finding himself bullied and made fun of often, Alejandro's creative outlet was of a more enterprising nature. "GoPed gas-powered scooters were all the rage at the time," Alejando recalls. "I found a hack where you could buy parts cheaply online and ended up selling them for a profit to the kids in my neighborhood." GoPed spare parts weren't the only things that Alejandro sold, and his side hustle extended to selling Starburst and Twix candies on the bus. "My father is an entrepreneur, and so was my grandfather from my mom's side, so I guess entrepreneurship has always been in my bloodline," Alejandro says.

Whether they knew it at the time, both Matt and Alejandro believed in the power of changing lives through storytelling. When it came time to enter college, Matt went to Northwestern University to study journalism, while Alejandro went to Harvard with plans of becoming an attorney, and eventually a US senator. What awaited them was anything but expected.

Matt started off by writing about what he knew best – music. He also started DJing to pursue a more solo musical endeavor. After a couple of years of attending shows weekly and covering different bands, an opportunity arose to spend a semester abroad in South Africa through a journalism residency. Matt leapt at it without hesitation. "Those six months in South Africa were one of the most incredible turning points of my life," Matt recalls. "I covered everything from the plight of street children to prison reform." In one of his more risky undertakings, Matt even made a trip to Harare, Zimbabwe, to cover the scenes from the challenge to Robert Mugabe's rule in the 2008 presidential election, without first informing his university nor his parents.

Getting to witness firsthand a level of poverty and hardship most of us are fortunate not to experience left Matt with two fresh thoughts. First, how his writing could be used for positive change, and second, how much more of the world he had yet to see and encounter. Matt spent a few years traveling and working out of the Asia Pacific region, but eventually decided to return to the US to study law at George Washington University as a way to move into human rights advocacy. This took Matt back to Africa, this time to Nigeria with an NGO focused on conflict resolution.

Part of Matt's time in Nigeria coincided with a two-week state of emergency, where he spent three months having to live on high alert and unbeknownst to him, falling sick each day from drinking unpurified water. Nonetheless, he still found time for his music. After befriending one of the biggest radio DJs in Nigeria, Matt even got the opportunity to play his music live on Nigerian radio to no less than six million listeners – an incredible experience only tempered by the reality of living a couple of blocks away from the center of a conflict zone. Those few months in Nigeria were an eye-opener. "I know I was just getting a small taste of what people there have to deal with every day," Matt says. "And while I still felt like there were ways I could help, I didn't necessarily feel like I could pursue all my passions with boots on the ground."

Before Matt even got far enough to contemplate his next steps, he found the most important email in his life waiting for him in his junk folder. Having still been writing the occasional article for music blogs, Matt's work had caught the eye of Kerri Mason, a journalist who had been covering dance music for *Billboard* at the time. Kerri, who was about to leave *Billboard*, was looking for her replacement. And from what she had seen of Matt's writing, he was the ideal candidate. Lo and behold – despite some large meandering turns, Matt's career path ended up returning him to what he had intended to be all along: a music journalist.

Once Matt joined *Billboard*, he never looked back, and went on to found the publication's dance and electronic music vertical, *Billboard Dance*, in 2015. At *Billboard*, Matt helped to shape dance culture by telling stories that resonated with millions of fans all around the world – from the highs of the meteoric rise of renowned DJs such as Kygo and the Chainsmokers to the lows of the tragic passing of Swedish DJ Avicii. It was during this time that Matt also got to DJ himself at some of the biggest EDM festivals, such as *EDC Japan* and *Tomorrowland*.

Music is widely regarded as the great connector – a nod to how it can create a shared universal feeling regardless of anyone's background. In Matt's case, however, that took a far more literal meaning, even though much more had to transpire before he and Alejandro met. In fact, while Matt's career was full of detours, Alejandro was busy navigating what felt more like a series of brutal start-stops.

Despite the accomplishment of getting into the most preeminent Ivy League, Harvard, just like everything else in Alejandro's life up until that point felt like a struggle. "My parents were at the time going through a divorce," Alejandro says. "I was also taking on two jobs to pay for school, on top of massive student loans." None of this felt particularly worthwhile especially after he got accused of and then suspended for plagiarism.

"I had misplaced or left out the parentheses that should accompany an author's name," Alejandro explains. "All of my citations were included in the bibliography, but I did not provide the author name or page number that you're supposed to have in the MLA format." MLA is a style of crediting sources commonly used in writing research papers.

With Alejandro's misdeed occurring not long after the widely publicized 2012 Harvard cheating scandal, where 125 students were charged with academic dishonesty after collaborating on a take-home final exam, leniency was out of the question despite complete lack of mal-intent on his part. Finding little reason or motivation to stay in Boston, Alejandro decided to drop out of Harvard. With just $300 to his name, Alejandro packed all of his belongings into two boxes and a backpack and moved to New York City. Once again, Alejandro found himself in survival mode and decided to take up a job in hospitality just to make ends meet.

"The access and opportunity you get by attending Harvard and even just having a harvard.edu email address is like having a cheat code that makes you feel unstoppable," Alejandro says. "While this was a soul-crushing job, I am also grateful that it brought me back down to earth and allowed me to relate to the experience of the everyday person." Because of that, Alejandro still counts his first job after dropping out of college as his most successful failure.

Eventually, Alejandro resigned, only to be approached by Elite Daily, an online news platform that was known for covering trending topics and putting out buzzy listicles targeted at millennials. While initially wary of being associated with the type of content Elite Daily, produced (Alejandro still had deep political aspirations and interests), Alejandro decided to join them as director of innovation and culture and ended up playing a critical role in not only diversifying the publication's content, but also leading the company to a $50M acquisition by British tabloid publication Daily Mail.

This was all that was needed to pave the way for the rest of Alejandro's professional career. After Elite Daily, Alejandro joined the corporate development team at Verizon, where he worked on strategic acquisitions and had a front row seat to billion-dollar deals such as the company's acquisition of AOL. It was also at Verizon that Alejandro got the opportunity to develop a deeper interest in emerging tech and in particular VR and AR. Alejandro eventually left to start his own creative agency focused on emerging tech and storytelling, as well as to found a nonprofit organization known as Oceanic Global.

It was through Oceanic Global that Alejandro and Matt were finally introduced by mutual friends. "Oceanic Global was organizing a conference in Ibiza and wanted to book the DJ Solomun," Matt recalls. "I was introduced to Alej as the person who knew all the DJs, and we became good friends soon after."

Over the next few years, Alejandro and Matt stayed in close and frequent communication even as they each worked on separate projects. Nonetheless, working together felt more of a when, not if. Drawing from his time and experience with strategic acquisitions at Verizon, Alejandro became Matt's trusted advisor when Matt was later in the process of navigating a sale of *Spin* magazine (which had earlier been acquired by Billboard) to private equity. Yet, unknown to Alejandro at the time, Matt was also starting to develop a deep and profound interest in something else altogether: NFTs.

Both Alejandro and Matt recall a time early in the pandemic when Alejandro had just moved to Jackson Hole, Wyoming, as a temporary retreat away from the city. "I invited Matt to unplug and be around nature, but instead all that came out of his mouth was NFT this and NFT that," Alejandro laughs.

Matt like many others at this time took to participating in NFT-related discussions on Clubhouse. Simultaneously, he decided to create @nftnow on both Twitter and Instagram, simply as a way to share art that he liked or newsworthy headlines about artists he had come across. "The whole thing was a journey of discovery for me, where I was sharing my learnings in real time," Matt says.

The nft now accounts started to grow in following and, more importantly, gained the attention of notable artists, including the likes of Los Angeles–based fine artist ThankYouX and electronic dance DJ 3LAU, whom Matt was already close friends with from his Billboard days. "When I told 3LAU and other folks that I was the one behind the nft now handles, they were all in disbelief and told me that I had to do more with it and build it into something that was more than just a social media account," Matt recalls.

As Matt continued to update Alejandro on his progress with nft now, it quickly became hard for either of them to unsee its potential. Together with a third cofounder Sam Hysell, a vision for a decentralized media company was born. "We have had a ten-year vision from day one," Alejandro says. "And that is to establish a new and better media model that does not rely on cookies or programmatic advertising for monetization, and fundamentally believes in user privacy as a human right."

nft now was quick to grow from a social media account with less than 10,000 followers run solely by Matt to establishing itself as a leading and authoritative voice in the NFT and broader Web3 space. To get there, Alejandro and Matt turned down millions of dollars along the way. "Every low effort profile picture (PFP) project or potential scam was trying to throw money at us for promotion, and we said no to all of them," Matt says. "One project based in Dubai tried to pay us $250,000 for a single tweet, but we knew our credibility was worth more than that."[2]

That discipline paid off, and within six months, nft now threw its first flagship event known as *Gateway* at Art Basel Miami, which they co-hosted with luxury auction house Christie's and attracted celebrity guests such as Jared Leto and Nile Rodgers. "For an organization like Christie's to work with a six-month-old start-up was a big deal," Matt says. "It opened a lot of doors for us and changed the nature of the conversations we were having."

Nonetheless, media businesses are notoriously one of the hardest to build, and even though this is neither Alejandro nor Matt's first rodeo in media, reimagining a century-old industry does not come without its challenges. As the market started to turn bearish in 2022, nft now like many others in the space had to resort to staff cuts – a difficult decision but one that was necessary to execute their long-term vision. "We went from being a media company covering Web3 to a media tech company powered by Web3," Matt explains. While nft now remains the company's flagship publication, it is housed under Now Media, which signifies both Matt and Alejandro's commitment to the future of onchain media.

"More so than ever, we need to be able to tell who wrote what," Alejandro says. "Especially in the age of AI when you have misinformation happening on a day-to-day basis." An economic study published by the University of Baltimore in 2019 revealed that fake news is estimated to cost the global economy $78 billion a year, a number that can only have increased given the rapid adoption of generative AI over the past couple of years.

"Putting media onchain allows publishers to attach their signature to content they are putting out on an immutable ledger," Alejandro continues. "This will allow us to hold publishers to a different level of integrity and standard of journalism." Matt adds, "We really do believe that Web2 media is broken, and simply a clickbait race to the bottom built on misaligned incentives." And while large media conglomerates may be slow to adopt such sweeping changes, both Matt and Alejandro feel it's only a matter of time before they do so.

"Throughout history, from the invention of the Gutenberg printing press to the emergence of dot-coms to eventually the rise of social media, publishers know they will need to adapt in order to survive," Matt says. "What we need to do is to keep building out our tech capabilities while also having the right conversations so publishers can understand that onchain authentication of content is more than just a nice to have."

Matt and Alejandro's vision for onchain media will not play out in time for the upcoming US presidential election cycle in 2024, in which misinformation is likely to once again play a role. That won't matter as both have their sights set on a far more distant future. "My legacy is not only going to be the values that I impart to my children," Alejandro says as he became a first-time father just last year. "It's about building the best possible world I can for them and children of their own." Getting there will take more than just the telling of Alejandro's or Matt's stories. What it will take is us demanding a change in the way the world tells all of ours.

6

Step 3: Get Your Hands Dirty

Now that you have identified your glow stick moment and found your why for wanting to dive further into Web3, it's time to roll up your sleeves and get to work.

As someone who has just moved halfway across the world, this will be reminiscent of similar inconveniences I faced when navigating my move (think: setting up a new bank account, retaking a driving test to get a new driver's license, getting a new mobile phone number, figuring out health insurance, etc.). My hope is that in the not too distant future, this particular chapter will be defunct, as that would mean we have all found a way to interact with the blockchain seamlessly.

#1: Get Social

What you'll need: X, Discord, and Farcaster (as a bonus!)

Community is such a large part of what Web3 is, because the core ethos stemming from its technological foundations is decentralization. That means a diversity of voices and opinions, though sometimes misguided, do make up a large part of one's experience in this nascent and rapidly evolving space.

I have found that the best way to truly immerse oneself in Web3 is to go ahead and be a part of the conversation, even if you aren't quite sure what to say just yet. For better or for worse, X is still the predominant home to most of this chatter, and the algorithm does a pretty good job of recommending interesting people to follow once you start populating your feed based on your interests.

Again, who to follow will depend very much on your glow stick moment and why, given how different the various subcommunities are in Web3. If you are into the digital art and NFT movement such as myself, the following are just a handful of names to get you started. And of course, I would also follow every single digital maverick that I have interviewed for this book.

- @thehugxyz: Official X account of HUG. Had to throw in a shameless plug, but more importantly, as home to tens of thousands of artists in Web3, we not only spotlight various creators worth discovering – we also share numerous art resources and opportunities weekly.
- @nftnow: A leading media publication that covers the latest not just in NFTs, but also in Web3, and AI.
- @CozomoMedici: A well-known pseudonymous digital art collector, who is the self-proclaimed "grand patron" of the digital art renaissance. Indeed, Cozomo has made the largest donation of onchain art to the Los Angeles County Museum of Art (LACMA). Cozomo also publishes a weekly newsletter, Medici Minutes, which covers interesting art developments in Web3.
- @Zeneca: A dear friend of mine, Zeneca (aka Roy Bhasin), is a former professional poker player turned thought leader in the crypto and NFT space. He is also the founder of a community called Zen Academy and has a great catalog of introductory articles to various Web3 concepts that can be found in his newsletter, *Letters from a Zeneca*.

- @ClaireSilver12: Claire is not only a preeminent AI artist who has been sold at Christie's and Sotheby's; she is also the cofounder of a nonprofit arts organization called Accelerate Art. Apart from constantly uplifting emerging artists, Claire also shares her very own tips on how to incorporate AI into your artistic practice.
- @betty_nft: Betty is the founder of an NFT community called Deadfellaz. Home to 10,000 variations of what is known as a profile picture (PFP), Deadfellaz is now leveraging its artwork IP (intellectual property) and turning it into a virtual trading card game. Betty often commentates on the current state of Web3 and does not shy away from difficult conversations around topics such as diversity and inclusion.

If you are ready to get extra adventurous, I also highly recommend you signing up for an account on Farcaster. As a one-liner, Farcaster is essentially a decentralized version of X. I go into further detail about it in Chapter 12, but for now, you can interpret it as a social media platform where everyone on there is deeply excited about the blockchain and what it has to offer. What you will find on Farcaster are the latest cutting-edge experiments and innovations on the blockchain, from bounty boards that connect available talent to gig work to onchain commerce that allow you to shop seamlessly with cryptocurrency.

Outside of X, conversations also take place on LinkedIn, and in various Discord servers (like that of Zen Academy's). Take some time to acquaint yourself with these platforms, and do not be afraid to make friends and ask questions.

#2: Do the Deed

What you'll need: Access to a cryptocurrency exchange[1] such as Coinbase and a non-custodial (sometimes also called self-custodial) wallet[2] such as Metamask.

What makes the entire Web3 onboarding process more complicated is the fact that there are many different cryptocurrencies. Just like how the US dollar, the euro, the Japanese yen, etc., all coexist, so too do Bitcoin, Ethereum, Solana, Avalanche, Tezos, and more.

Nonetheless, it's time to get hold of your very own cryptocurrency and start using it. First off, start by figuring out what you want to do with it. For illustrative purposes, say you are looking to use cryptocurrency to purchase digital art as an NFT. The standard process would then look as follows:

1. Figure out which blockchain you are looking to purchase your NFT on, and hence which cryptocurrency you need.
2. Purchase the cryptocurrency on a crypto exchange that operates in your country. Common ones include Coinbase, Crypto.com, and Kraken. Because the exchange still has control over your funds (similar to how a traditional bank holds your money), your funds are referred to as being held in a custodial wallet.[3]
3. To be able to transact with NFT marketplaces, you will more likely than not need to set up a non-custodial wallet (examples include Coinbase Wallet, Metamask, Rainbow Wallet, and Phantom), which would involve you jotting down a series of random words (known as a seed phrase), which serve as your private keys to access it.
4. Transfer the cryptocurrency you have purchased from your exchange to your non-custodial wallet.
5. Connect your non-custodial wallet to the NFT marketplace where the NFT you would like to purchase is listed.
6. Purchase the NFT, as you would in a standard e-commerce transaction. In some cases, the NFT will be transferred from the seller's wallet to yours. In others, this transaction will result in the NFT being created on the blockchain, and hence being "minted" to your wallet.

Anyone can see that the process above is tedious and off-putting. Further, what decentralization offers us in terms of true ownership is completely offset by inconvenience and lack of usability.

While consumers are by and large expecting to be able to trust crypto exchanges, FTX was one glaring example of how that trust would have been sorely misplaced. In that instance, keeping your cryptocurrency in FTX (and hence in their custodial wallet) offered convenience but rendered the funds unrecoverable when the exchange later went bankrupt.

Conversely, transferring funds into a non-custodial wallet would give the user full control over their funds but would require the user to jot down and keep safe their own seed phrase. No one will have jurisdiction over those funds, but that also means there is no recourse should that seed phrase get lost or compromised.

This points to real usability issues in Web3, all of which are being actively worked on. For example, companies such as MoonPay make it easy for one to purchase cryptocurrency directly to their non-custodial wallet with their credit card, bypassing steps 2–4.

Similarly, real innovation is also occurring on the blockchain level. For example, Ethereum's newly launched ERC-4337 token standard effectively turns one's wallet into a smart contract account.[4] Without worrying too much about the technical jargon, what this effectively means is that users can through this technology access their wallets via more familiar methods such as email/password, and two-factor authentication (2FA).

So while the current process is imperfect, owning cryptocurrency of your own is a standard course of action you'll need to take to fully experience Web3 at work.

Further, when transferring cryptocurrency or an NFT from one wallet to another, you will get to see firsthand how they truly are "magical teleporting pieces of paper," given that they happen almost instantaneously with low or minimal fees. Now, imagine other use cases, such as moving money across bank accounts or transferring a car deed from seller to buyer, and how much those could be meaningfully enhanced through blockchain technology.

#3: Safety First

What you'll need: High level of vigilance and skepticism, Wallet Guard browser extension, a hardware wallet (Ledger, Trezor)

You've got pretty much almost everything you need, but before that, you need a safety briefing. Unfortunately, Web3 is still very much rampant with scams and bad actors. This means that there is often someone trying to circulate a nefarious link, be it in a private message, or via a public post on X or Discord.

Similar to anything you have read about email phishing scams, always be careful before clicking on any links. Never give your seed phrase to anybody, and double-check and triple-check (i) what site you are connecting your wallet to, and (ii) what transactions you are authorizing. One handy tool to consider is Wallet Guard, which is a browser extension that alerts you to malicious websites and simulates the outcome of transactions you are signing before you do so.

In the event that you have accidentally given a malicious website access to your wallet when you did not intend to, visit revoke.cash immediately to revoke access. When something like this happens, you should then also transfer out your assets to a brand-new wallet that has not yet been compromised.

Lastly, should you end up holding a large amount of cryptocurrency or highly valued NFTs, you may also consider investing in a hardware wallet, such as Ledger or Trezor. Hardware wallets act more as a storage vault and should never be used for any transactions.

Again, anything that comes with such a huge warning label is hardly prime for mass adoption. Nonetheless, it is par for the course for a maverick to move forth in such unchartered waters. So onwards!

Your Web3 Toolkit Checklist

As opposed to writing prompts, this chapter is accompanied by a checklist to make sure you have taken sufficient action to commence your journey as a digital maverick. While you do not have to do every single thing on this checklist (let us be real – social media can be especially overwhelming), the more you do, the more acquainted you will be with this unfamiliar world of Web3.

Separately, do not forget to reflect on your experience along the way. What was difficult or easy about each thing on the checklist? What did you not understand? Were there things that made you feel unwelcome, and did you feel like giving up at some point? Take note of these to identify friction points to shed some light on not only how early we are, but also where you could make an impact.

Get social

- ☐ Set up an account and follow 100 Web3 content creators in X.
- ☐ Join at least one but no more than three Discord servers to connect with other communities.
- ☐ Get Telegram and look out for relevant Telegram groups to join.
- ☐ Sign up for an account on Farcaster, and join in the conversation on its client Warpcast (learn more in Chapter 12).
- ☐ Sign up for an account on HUG . . . if you are an artist or art lover!

Do the deed

- ☐ Purchase cryptocurrency via a cryptocurrency exchange, e.g. Coinbase, Binance, Kraken.

(continued)

(*continued*)

- ☐ Set up a non-custodial wallet, such as Metamask, Rainbow, Phantom.
- ☐ Purchase an NFT on an NFT marketplace such as Magic Eden, Rarible, Nifty Gateway, or OpenSea.
- ☐ Experiment with different blockchains by onboarding yourself to Bitcoin, Ethereum, and one other blockchain such as Tezos or Solana to understand how different ecosystems operate.
- ☐ Experience a fiat on ramp to crypto by purchasing crypto. You can do so through service providers such as MoonPay, which is accessible directly from the self-custodial wallets listed above.
- ☐ Experience a custodial wallet solution by collecting and customizing an avatar on Reddit.

Safety first

- ☐ Set up a hardware wallet, such as Ledger, and transfer blockchain assets in and out of it.
- ☐ Install a browser extension such as Wallet Guard to safeguard you from malicious sites.

***

> **MEET A MAVERICK: How Shavonne Wong Is Modeling Human and Cultural Identity in a Digital Future**
>
> Shavonne Wong is a Singaporean digital artist and 3D virtual model creator with a background in fashion and advertising photography. Her work, recognized in *Forbes* 30 Under 30 Asia in 2020, often features life-like virtual models in surreal digital landscapes. Shavonne's brand collaborations include the likes of Vogue Singapore and Bang & Olufsen. Her work has also been sold at Sotheby's and includes collectors such as actor Idris Elba.

Millennials may remember with nostalgia the reality TV show hosted by supermodel Tyra Banks, *America's Next Top Model* (often abbreviated as *ANTM*). The long-running competition series, while never having quite reached the popularity of other shows such as *Survivor* and *American Idol*, nonetheless helped to define the reality TV genre, which was just starting to emerge at the time.

Whatever you may make of the Top Model franchise, especially through the lens of today, it was successful enough to result in several international spin-offs. And as someone like Shavonne Wong who remembers watching season 1 of *ANTM* as a teenager from thousands of miles away in Singapore, it was a dream come true when she got to become a guest photographer for *Asia's Next Top Model* over a decade later.

As a fellow Singaporean, I've always been in awe of what Shavonne has been able to accomplish as a professional creative. For two people born just two years apart and growing up in the same small society that was decidedly conservative and pragmatic, our outlooks and approaches to life could not have been more different, especially as young adults. Funnily enough, I too remember watching season 1 of *ANTM*, and while I had never aspired to a career in fashion, I recall myself wanting to give singing a good go when *Singapore Idol* made its way to our shores.

I doubt I would have been good enough in spite of my choir chops, but the difference between Shavonne and I is that I never even tried. In fact, I do not think for one second I ever thought that a creative career was a viable one until three years ago (read: when I was introduced to Web3).

Yet, Shavonne's and my upbringings were more similar than I expected, in that we were both raised as the younger of two siblings by strict tiger moms. "My mom was a super tiger mom," Shavonne says. "She was the one that my friends' parents would reference when they wanted to discourage their own children from behaving poorly." Indeed, both Shavonne and I have a shared experience of not being allowed out very much, having strict curfews, and, being forced by our moms, compelled to learn how to play the piano for nearly 10 years despite not having much innate skill nor interest in it.

At some point however, Shavonne's and my paths started to diverge. After completing secondary school at age 16, Shavonne opted for polytechnic education over junior college, which she dismissed as a "harder version of secondary school." For those less familiar, the difference between these two tertiary education pathways in Singapore was that polytechnics emphasized real-world application and industry-specific skills, while junior colleges tended to focus on deeper theoretical learning in specific academic disciplines. Indeed, while Shavonne was picking up what I consider to be way more practical skills such as animation and computer programming as part of her IT degree, I was deep in my reading about the French Revolution and busy dissecting poems by William Blake.

Shavonne's foray into fashion photography came to her by chance however. Soon after graduation, she found herself flipping through a fashion magazine and spuriously wanting to give fashion photography a go. "Within a week, I borrowed a camera, rented a studio, and dragged my sister there to be my first-ever model," Shavonne recalls. "After three to four more photoshoots, which I got my friends to model in, I started putting together a portfolio and reaching out to other freelance models and makeup artists that were also just starting out."

From there, Shavonne describes her photography career as continuing to develop organically. "My first few jobs were all with fashion design students who needed to hire a photographer for their work," Shavonne tells me. "Then, it progressed to me shooting for young start-up designers who were starting their own brand, and before I knew it, I was working on campaigns for international brands like Sephora and Lancôme." As it turned out, working on *Asia's Next Top Model* was just one of Shavonne's many achievements over the next 10 years. She got to shoot award-winning actor and singer Billy Porter for *Vogue*, and was also recognized as a *Forbes* 30 Under 30 recipient.

Throughout this time and till today, Shavonne's mantra for herself is to just wing it, which she acknowledges was only possible through the support of her parents, whom she continued to live with after polytechnic. "At the start of my career, I wasn't earning enough to really feed myself, and it took a long time to see any form of financial return ... but I recognize that I had the opportunity to keep experimenting and learning because I still had a home and food on the table to go back to thanks to my parents," Shavonne says.

Nonetheless, it's clear that parental support alone would not have been sufficient to get Shavonne to where she did. It was rather the willingness to show up and wing it, as Shavonne likes to say, that did. "Nobody knows what the f*** they are doing most of the time. The more people I've worked with, the more I've realized that most of us are just trying to do our best and see what happens from there ... so just go out there and wing it."

Winging it came in an even bigger way for Shavonne once the pandemic set in. COVID made it impossible for her to shoot with real fashion models, and so Shavonne did the next best thing – make her own. She spent all of 2020 picking up 3D modeling from watching YouTube videos, starting with the most basic of tutorials where she learned how to make a donut from a 3D artist named Andrew Price, who also goes by the name Blender Guru. Shavonne soon progressed from making donuts to constructing virtual models, which she created so that she could eventually pitch them to her fashion clients.

While 3D art is a medium that Shavonne describes as a "complete pain" (with each piece taking her anywhere from weeks to months), and one that differs vastly from fashion photography, her passion for both mediums was born out of her desire to conjure scenes directly from her imagination. "Most other photography is built around the idea of documentation . . . such as documenting your reality, your city, your landscape," Shavonne says. "With fashion photography, I was always drawn to the idea that I could create whatever I want, and tell a story with the craziest of sets, makeup, styling, etc." To Shavonne, creating her own virtual models simply stretched the possibilities of what she could do, especially when they were at the time being limited by lockdowns and social distancing regulations.

It wasn't long before Shavonne's 3D creations found their way to the blockchain, which she credits very much to her husband, who had already been working in crypto for a few years. Even though he had first mentioned NFTs to her in late 2019, Shavonne did not mint and sell her first works on the blockchain till February 2021. "My husband would tell me all about crypto, and I was just the supportive wife making sounds of approval even though I never really took any interest in it," Shavonne laughs.

All that changed once Shavonne decided to dive into crypto X (which is still more colloquially referred to Crypto Twitter, or CT for short) herself and to her surprise, found a like-minded community of open-minded and creative people. "What I found most attractive about NFTs was that it had this group of people who were excited about trying new things . . . all while the world around us was falling apart," Shavonne says. "That checked a lot of boxes for me, and I found it super fun to be meeting people from all over the world to talk about this weird and insane space."

Through NFTs, Shavonne was eventually introduced to independent art curator and fellow Singaporean Clara Peh. The two of them clicked instantly, and together with two other cofounders, decided to found a community of Asia-based and Asian artists called NFT Asia in March 2021. "I had been in the space for about two months, and realized that even though Asia makes up the majority of the world, there were very few Asians that were actively engaging as part of the global NFT community," Shavonne says.

With that, Shavonne and Clara wanted NFT Asia to be a space where the Asian creative community could feel comfortable and at home. "There's a huge difference growing up in Asia and growing up in the West when it comes to the level of outspokenness, and what is considered polite or rude . . . and in this space, if you do not speak out, you do not get heard," Shavonne says. "We created NFT Asia to not only showcase the artistic talent that we have in Asia, but also to demonstrate that Asian artists create more than just 'Asian-looking art.'" In just three short years, NFT Asia has gone on to showcase their artists in exhibitions all over the world, from New York to Dubai.

The opportunities that NFT Asia has provided to its stable of emerging artists are not the only ones that have been made possible by Web3. Shavonne credits a lot of her own career highlights to NFTs as well, such as having her work collected by actor Idris Elba and getting to work on the first NFT cover for *Vogue* magazine, which she got through a cold outreach to its editor. "This to me is why it's good to be early," Shavonne explains. "Am I the best virtual model creator in the world? Maybe one day, but not yet. The only reason why I got this opportunity is because I am in a space that has less competition and less saturation of people doing the same thing."

Shavonne's comment struck me that even though we may have pursued vastly different career paths, there's still something about a Singapore upbringing that instills in us a sense of realism and pragmatism – something that Shavonne has carried with her long before NFTs. "Every creative typically starts off very idealistic, believing that if you do good work, they will come," Shavonne says. "That is just not true. There is no spotlight that will miraculously find you as you are walking down the street . . . and to bank your entire career on the lottery of life makes no practical sense."

"If you are an artist that does not care about selling your work or being in the limelight, then by all means, do whatever you want. But do not be an artist that wants fame and recognition, and then not want to market yourself," Shavonne continues. "If you want to be able to say that you have a career that you love – which is not something that many people can say in their lifetime – then you also have to be able to accept the bad parts and all the things you do not enjoy with it."

After three short years of becoming a fine artist, Shavonne is actively working on refining her artistic voice and having her work reflect her interest in society, specifically how we view identity and personhood in a digital future. Having spent her entire life in Singapore, she has recently decided to move to Bangkok, Thailand, in hope that a new environment will expand her views and the way she does her art.

Tyra Banks famously sings in the *ANTM* opening theme song, "Wanna Be on Top?" And while many may answer yes to that question, few like Shavonne understand the necessary and practical steps required to get there (Figure 6.1).

Figure 6.1 One of Shavonne Wong's 3D artworks from her *Love is Love* collection.

Source: With permission of Shavonne Wong.

7

Step 4: Transfer Your Skills

AFTER SERVING OUT my bond, i.e. working for the Singapore government for six years in return for them paying for my college education, I knew it was time for a change. Sure, I had ventured into entrepreneurship in the boutique fitness space with my indoor cycling business, but that was ultimately still considered a side hustle (albeit a very stressful one).

I also knew that I wanted to leave the world of finance. It paid well; so much so that by leaving it, I knew that I would be leaving plenty of money on the table. In fact, I estimate forgoing at least $1 million in pay in the five years since I've quit being a full-time investor (yes, Wall Street is every bit as outrageous as it proclaims to be).

Immediately, I recognize the privilege I have in being able to say money is not the singular most important thing to me. Yet, beyond making enough to pay the bills and afford some lifestyle inflation that has come with placing one-too-many Uber Eats orders, what was most important to me was continuing to expand my skill set and being able to apply it to problems and missions that excited me.

During this time, I thought long and hard about becoming a full-time founder and entrepreneur. At the same time, I did not really have an idea I felt sufficiently convinced about, and felt I still had much to learn after my experience with 7Cycle.

It was during this time that I found myself landing a job in the world of live sports – in a Mixed Martial Arts (MMA) promotion, no less. Called ONE Championship (aka ONE), the company was UFC's biggest rival in Asia, and went on to be home to a number of UFC world champions, including 15x Flyweight World Champion Demetrious Johnson, who truly is the nicest and yet most lethal fighter you'll ever meet.

Looking back, it's wild that ONE's founder and CEO, Chatri Sityodtong, took a chance on hiring me as his chief of staff. Up till then, I had a deskbound job crunching numbers, reading and analyzing company quarterly filings, and making my best-informed predictions on how much a publicly traded company was worth through my "highly scientific" financial models. I knew close to nothing about MMA outside of Conor McGregor and had never practiced any form of martial arts outside of taking a couple of recreational Muay Thai lessons.

In a matter of weeks, I was responsible for expanding ONE's business in Japan, sitting in stuffy boardrooms across long-time Japanese media executives negotiating sponsorship and media rights deals, while also costing out our stadium events (who knew how much stadium LEDs cost!) and fight cards.

When I entered the world of Web3, all of this was a great reminder to myself that all skills are more transferable than you think. In fact, I've come to find that one of the biggest misconceptions people have about Web3 and crypto is that you have to be a deeply technical person to find a role in it.

That could not be further from the truth.

Especially in Web3, where everyone is still figuring things out as they go, I have found this saying to be true. *No one really knows what they are doing until they have done it.*

As you have gone about identifying your glow stick moment, understanding your why, and getting your hands dirty interacting with the blockchain, the next step is figuring out what skills you have that can benefit this growing community of voracious learners and experimenters.

These skills can be more out of left field than you think. I have to look no further than the exemplary team I work with every day. My marketing manager, Tina Survilla Lindell, is a trained sociolinguist, who took her linguistic skills into refugee education and medical copywriting, before now running social media marketing and product copywriting here at HUG. The very same skills she acquired from breaking down health care jargon ended up being highly relevant in making blockchain technology appear less daunting for artists new to Web3.

Or consider Kevin Sonei, better known as kmoney, an LA-based commercial director whose career as a comedian found added traction once he found a niche in creating comedic Web3 content only crypto degenerates[1] found amusing.

Without a doubt, some of the most inspiring stories come from the artists I work with daily. Jimena Buena Vida, a Colombian-born artist now residing in the US, was a computer science engineer for years before she found deeper fulfillment in taking her JavaScript coding knowledge and applying it to the field of generative art. Today, Jimena is the artist behind several sold-out collections of colorful, modern, abstract art all created from code. NFTs allowed her to not only connect with a global audience for her art that she would otherwise not have found from the traditional art world, but also to monetize and make a living from doing what she loves most – create.

When I reflect on my earliest days in Web3 before HUG, I took the skills I acquired from my finance days of learning how to synthesize large amounts of information into bite-sized chunks and shared that with the NFT community on X through what was then called Twitter threads. That took me from being an absolute nobody and novice to someone with not just something to say, but something to offer.

More importantly, you never know when the right person may start to look or take notice. After about a month of sharing my learnings on X and connecting with others in the community, I was convinced that Web3 was where I needed to next take my career.

As luck would have it, so did Randi Zuckerberg, who already had more career accolades than most people do in their lifetime. Having spent her past year mentoring a handful of founders of NFT communities, she was looking for a ~~co-conspirator~~ cofounder to execute her vision of helping more artists become entrepreneurs through the power of blockchain technology.

Those Twitter threads that I had started writing as a way of journaling my learnings, in hope that they would also be beneficial to someone else new to Web3, were better than any résumé I could have put together. They demonstrated that I had a point of view, a vision, and also a desire to make Web3 better than when I found it.

Believe it or not, you likely have one too. Regardless of how new you are to the world of Web3, there will undoubtedly be something about it that you'd like to fix and improve. And chances are, you already have the skills to do so. This is why identifying your glow stick moment in Step 1 is so important, because the right glow stick will also be a powerful but nagging thought or idea you are unable to shake.

With that, reflect on your own personal journey, and how your skills (be it marketing, communication, community building, operations, etc.) can find a home in the Wild, Wild West of Web3. Then, apply and transfer them, and see what doors they open for you.

How to Combine Your Skills and Interests into Your Ikigai

Ikigai is a Japanese concept that refers to giving a person a sense of purpose or reason for living.

Popularized in recent times, it is about finding the intersection of what you love, what you are good at, what the world needs, and what you can be paid for. We already know that the world needs a better Internet in the form of Web3, which leaves you with three other areas to identify in order to find your ikigai.

Identifying your skills and interests is the first part of that process. After all, the better you are at something, the more likely you will open yourself up to financial opportunity.

Let us start with identifying your skills:

- Make a list of all the skills you believe you possess. Think broadly, so that this can include both hard skills such as any certifications you may already have, as well as soft skills such as communication or management skills.
- Evaluate each of these skills and rate your level of proficiency in each of them. More importantly, identify the skills that you particularly enjoy having, as what we are good at does not always align with what excites us. For example, I am adept at financial modeling but it's not something that I particularly look forward to doing.
- It can be hard at times to identify your own skills. The easiest hack? Ask your friends, family, or coworkers to share their observations about your skills with you. Invite them to be frank and honest with you, and if

(continued)

(continued)

    possible, provide examples of when they have seen those skills in practice.
- Consider taking a variety of skills assessment tests or quizzes. Related to these are also popular personality tests such as an enneagram test, which can make you aware of any predispositions you may have, especially when it comes to dealing with certain situations or groups of people.

The process for identifying your interests is remarkably similar to identifying your skills if only a little bit more introspective.

- Make a list of activities or topics you enjoy. What are you naturally drawn to? Even if you spend a lot of time doomscrolling through Instagram Reels or TikTok videos, which topics fascinate you and hold your attention span that bit longer?
- Challenge yourself to evaluate each interest and how they could relate to a career. Take it one step further by looking at common job roles in Web3 and see which ones overlap with your passions.

Once you have a good sense of what your skills and interests are, bring it all together. Do not forget your why for exploring Web3, and reach out to people who share in your why and passions to learn how they are applying their strengths to push the industry forward. Start this process of transferring your skills now, and you too will become an expert before you know it.

***

> **MEET A MAVERICK: How Jimena Buena Vida Is Decoding Her Life's Purpose through Art and Motherhood**
>
> Jimena Buena Vida is a Colombian-born computer science engineer turned artist whose work merges art, emotions, and technology. Her geometric and colorful explorations are a manifestation of her mission to inspire transformation and human connection through vulnerability and self-awareness. Jimena's work blends analog and digital approaches, and infuses painting and animation with the prowess of JavaScript code. Jimena has several sold-out collections on multiple blockchains and has also had her work exhibited worldwide.

On December 7, 2023, Hungarian-born artist Vera Molnár, who is widely known as the godmother of generative art, died at the age of 99. Generative art, otherwise known as creative coding, algorithmic art, or perhaps even more simply known as "computer art," is an art form that emerged in the mid-1960s but has arguably found growing relevance and popularity in the advent of blockchain technology. Much of this has been due to the emergence of Art Blocks, a generative art NFT platform launched by Erick "Snowfro" Calderon in 2021, which then borne its first collection on the blockchain, *Chromie Squiggles*.

Since then, Art Blocks has become home to several iconic generative art collections by artists such as Snowfro himself, Tyler Hobbs, and Dmitri Cherniak, all incredible artists who have had their works fetch millions of dollars. Amid all the sensational headlines about sales numbers, contributions to advance the field of generative art from predecessors such as Molnár, who was one of the first women to use computers in her art practice, stayed relatively unknown in the Web3 space. This only started to change in the handful of years leading up to her death, when Molnár exhibited at the Venice Biennale in 2022.

I speak of Molnár because her legacy will forever be tied to the origins of generative art. In a similar fashion, my hope is for Colombian-born artist Jimena Buena Vida's to be a part of its future.

Jimena was born in Bogotá to a mother who was the youngest of 14, which meant that Jimena's childhood was reminiscent of large family gatherings of 60–80 people. Her grandmother, who was the matriarch of the family and whom Jimena describes as insightful and hilarious, was also an early source of inspiration to her. "My grandmother owned and managed her own hotel, while my grandfather traveled as a farmer," Jimena recalls. "Cooking and bringing loved ones together over food was huge for her, and the idea of making and creating something from scratch that other people could enjoy was always something that resonated with me."

Despite growing up in a lively and dynamic household, things were not necessarily smooth sailing for Jimena. Raised by her mother after her parents divorced when she was two, Jimena witnessed firsthand the resilience and determination it took to be a single parent. "We moved a lot, and I changed schools more times than I can remember," Jimena says. "I understood that my mom was on a personal journey while caring for me, and while her unwavering dedication was always evident, it wasn't without its share of loneliness and challenges."

Eventually, Jimena's mom followed in her own mother's footsteps and found joy in opening up her own small restaurant, which Jimena describes as a turning point for them. "I was really inspired seeing my mom's journey of becoming a business owner, where she poured her heart and soul into all the things that came with running her own business such as bookkeeping and supplier management," Jimena tells me. It was also in her mom's restaurant that Jimena developed a strong work ethic of her own, where she waited tables to earn her keep.

When Jimena turned 16, the point at which most students graduate from high school in Colombia, she was faced with a pivotal decision of her own. "Survival was always so front and center for me," Jimena recalls. "For the majority of my life, I felt that there was a tiger chasing me, and every decision I made was to prevent me from getting eaten." So even though Jimena had little knowledge of what career she wanted to pursue, she took up one of her cousin's suggestions to study computer science in college. "All I cared about was whether I was going to be able to pay the bills after graduating," Jimena says.

Yet, Jimena described her college experience as "incredibly painful." Unbeknownst to her at the time, Jimena was neurodivergent and suffered from dyslexia, which made it difficult for her to see a project to completion within the traditional confines of a classroom environment. Jimena also contemplated dropping out of computer science in favor of more creative pursuits she enjoyed, such as painting and playing the piano, but ultimately persevered and graduated with a degree in software engineering.

Over the next few years, Jimena dabbled in a few different roles, including consulting for small businesses while also teaching online courses in HTML and SQL to underrepresented communities in state colleges. While these endeavors ensured financial stability as she had intended, Jimena also felt ready for the next adventure. It was then that she decided to apply for a master's degree in Southern Illinois University in the United States.

Moving to the US for graduate school was an unexpectedly amazing experience for Jimena, considering what she had gone through in college. "I found immersing myself in another culture very beautiful. It was the first time I had met people from other countries like Saudi Arabia, China, Korea, and Brazil, and it opened my eyes to the diversity of human experience from all around the world," Jimena says.

Jimena wanted to stay in the US after graduation, but as any international students (myself included) will know, the path to permanent residency is anything but straightforward. Jimena applied to what felt like hundreds of jobs and faced countless rejections from employers not willing to sponsor her work visa.

But once again, Jimena's perseverance paid off, and she managed to land an internship that eventually paved the way for a long-term work visa and eventually a green card.

Jimena ended up spending eight years in corporate America, with a large portion of her time being spent at Mastercard helping South American banking clients adopt EMV chip technology over the then more widely used magnetic stripes. Eventually, Jimena married and found a new life calling – motherhood – and decided to quit her job to become a stay-at-home mom. "I wanted to be there for my daughters during the crucial early years that shape their characters," Jimena says. "I also know how fortunate I am to have had enough savings and a supportive husband to be able to make that decision."

While Jimena has no regrets, she also describes being a stay-at-home mom as one of the hardest things that she has ever done. "It was a hard transition going from a nine-to-five job to having one that is essentially 24/7," Jimena tells me. "I learned how easy it is to feel overwhelmed and burned out, and how important it is to pause and make time for self-care."

Yet, as challenging as motherhood is, it was the opportunity to parent that reintroduced art into Jimena's life. "When the pandemic hit, I had to homeschool my daughters, and so I started making space for them to create," Jimena says. "When I saw them painting and creating artworks in a way that felt so natural to them, it suddenly made me question why I had been so much in my own head all this time."

Jimena started to incorporate mindfulness practices into her life, including Wim Hof breathing exercises, which involve taking deep breaths and holding them for increasingly longer periods of time. At some point, Jimena describes herself as having "literal visions of art," which she started turning into physical paintings of her own. Creating art allowed Jimena to shake what must have felt like self-inhibiting thoughts her entire life. "I realized the tiger that I had been afraid of had gone to bed a long time ago, and that there is no one chasing me now," Jimena says.

Jimena, who till today remains inspired by both her mom's and grandmother's entrepreneurial spirit, decided to turn her art practice into a side hustle. She started listing her paintings for sale online, and even approached local coffee shops in St Louis, Missouri, where she and her family currently reside, to see if anyone would let her hang and sell her paintings off their walls.

As Jimena continued looking for different ways to find buyers for her art, she perked up as soon as she read about Beeple's headline grabbing $69M NFT sale. Wanting to learn more, Jimena was surprised how few resources there were about NFTs at the time. She eventually found a podcast featuring an interview with mixed media artist Anne Spalter talking about NFTs. Without hesitation, Jimena slid into Spalter's DMs on Instagram asking for guidance. To her surprise, not only did Spalter respond to her message, but she also offered to jump on a 30-minute call to share whatever she knew to Jimena.

From her initial conversation with Spalter, Jimena discovered more artist role models in Web3 such as Luisa Salas, a Mexican artist and muralist, eventually making her way to and discovering a community of Web3 artists and collectors on Clubhouse. Jimena recalls of those early days, "I would have a headset in one ear listening to a Clubhouse conversation about NFTs, while leaving the other ear open to tend to my daughters and even potty train my youngest."

Over time and together with her newfound learnings of NFTs, Jimena was inspired to take her JavaScript coding knowledge from her computer science days and bring them into her physical paintings. Not only did this open Jimena up to entirely new mediums of generative art and also animation, but it also introduced her to an ever-growing collector base on the blockchain.

In January 2024, Jimena made waves across the crypto art community when she became the first artist to mint on the RARI chain, a new blockchain built by Rarible that honors creator royalties. Titled Nefarious Meditation, the artwork was created with p5.js[2] (a JavaScript programming library for creative coding) and featured an animated visual of evolving gradients in a grid. Per Jimena, its aim was to draw its viewers into a meditative experience that simulates a child-like state . . . not unlike what Jimena herself first witnessed when she saw her daughters making art during the pandemic. Nefarious Meditation alone has been collected by nearly 13,000 people.

Yet, in spite of the reputational and financial success Jimena has found as an artist in Web3, she stays mindful of what it takes to weather the ups and downs. "I recognized early on that this space is built like a casino, and with that comes a high risk of compromising your well-being," Jimena says. "So while the volatility is unavoidable, I knew that I had to understand my worth as an artist and a human, independent of what goes on in crypto, and accordingly, when and how to disconnect from the noise."

"If you are constantly measuring your self-worth by your sales figures or the speed of your success, or if you are constantly comparing yourself to others you see on social media, you will never find true happiness," Jimena adds. "It's also not about the latest meta, or what others are doing. For me, it's about having the courage to keep creating and sharing my art, which is a reflection of who I am and what is intrinsic in me since the day I was born."

Today, Jimena describes her work as one that inspires transformation and human connection through vulnerability and self-discovery. But this mission is not just evident in her colorful abstract creations. It is embodied in Jimena everywhere she goes.

"Engaging with this online community of artists and builders, and then getting to meet them face-to-face is one of the best things I've experienced," Jimena says, despite her numerous career highlights already including a solo show in New York City and numerous sold out art collections that predates Nefarious Meditation.

Jimena understands that it can be daunting for anyone to get their start in Web3. "In the last three years, I've shown up to events and to spaces even when I have not been invited, and even when I felt I did not yet belong," Jimena says. "But I kept showing up with my integrity, my energy, and my confidence, and realized it wasn't just me, but many others who have been willing to show up with their fears and imperfections. It is this serendipitous energy that has created the community we have today."

Nearly seven years after quitting her job to be a stay-at-home mom for her daughters, Jimena is now a full-time working artist. With her children having been the source of inspiration for Jimena to pursue her love for art, she naturally hopes to inspire them with life lessons of her own. "I just want them to know that there are no shortcuts and that you can accomplish anything you put your mind to. And that last of all, no matter what you have gone through, you can always improve your life if you really want to," Jimena says.

When Vera Molnár passed, Jimena created a tribute art piece titled Eternity, a p5.js animation accompanied with the words "In a breath, eternity lies, timeless and vast, a dance in the skies, forever to advance." Whether Jimena knows it yet, her eternity in the form of a legacy to both her daughters and her craft is too just beginning (Figure 7.1).

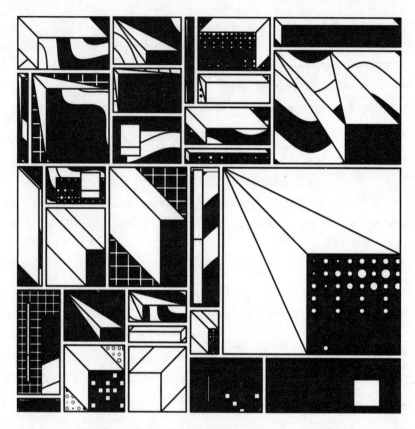

Figure 7.1 *All Our Faces #2* **by Jimena Buena Vida.**
Source: With permission of Jimena Cecilia Wissehr.

8

Step 5: Join a Cabal . . . or Make Your Own

MEMES ARE A funny thing. While it's a term popularized by the Internet, linguists argue that humans have used memes to communicate for centuries. Social commentators have attempted to describe memes in a variety of ways, from a "self-replicating chunk of information" or "an idea that rips through the public consciousness." Either way, whether we like or understand it, today's culture is fueled by memes.

Unsurprisingly, Web3 flourishes on memes of its own. After all, as shared in the *New York Times* article titled "The Meaning and History of Memes," "creating and sharing memes facilitates a sense of community online while maintaining a feeling of exclusivity." That feeling of community juxtaposed with exclusivity could not sum up Web3 better.

The day after Christmas in 2023, a popular X content creator and Spaces (X's social audio chat rooms that now rival Clubhouse) host who goes by the name Leap posted this on X.

> *There is an inner circle/cabal that exists within web3. This is not an equal playing field.*

Time to break it down.

1. *Token cabal: these are group chats that share alpha[1] about erc/spl tokens that people are buying.*

    But what they don't tell you, is that it's usually someone in the chat who is actually making the coins.

    Yes you can absolutely make money buying these calls early, but it's important to understand that you are exit liquidity.[2]

2. *NFT cabal: there's a group of nft "influencers" that get allowlist for every mint. Usually it's in return for posting about the project.[3]*

    Sometimes you'll see this commonly with projects that create honorary pfps for people.

3. *Angel check cabal: there's a group of influencers who get contacted by every infrastructure project or new dapp [decentralized application] that's being built.[4]*

    These influencers are typically asked to write a check for anywhere from 5k to 25k usd and in return will be named as advisor for the project and receive tokens at a much lower valuation.

Now that we've gotten that out of the way, I can move on to the good news.

Admittedly, I am kind of in all these cabals, but you can be too. I started in web3 by myself, with absolutely zero outside/inside connections or networks.

Literally anyone can put in the work to build these networks for themselves. It's difficult, but very possible.

Every person who's successful in this industry has one thing in common. They all have more information than the baseline web3 participant. Information is the most valuable asset you can have here.

Of the 270 words in that post, it was the word "cabal" that became an instant meme . . . so much so that Beeple (the artist best known for making art every single day for 16+ years, and selling the compilation of his first 5,000 days as an NFT for a record-breaking $69M) created one of his daily artworks in reference to it.

Elsewhere on X, responses ranged from amused to disgusted. After all, as Betty, the founder of the Deadfellaz NFT community, put it, "Group chats are not cabals, guys. This is jpegs not global politics."

Cabal or group chat, what Leap's post meant to highlight was the amount of information asymmetry that is prevalent in Web3. Whether one was speculating in memecoins, NFTs, or tokens being issued by a Web3 start-up, his point was that you would likely be at the losing end of a trade if you were not already in the know by being in one of these so-called cabals.

The other point Leap was trying to make was that, unlike in more traditional industries, anyone can network their way into becoming a part of a cabal. While ironic since this seems to reinforce a sense of elitism that Web3 purports to shy away from, Leap is not entirely wrong. After all, many of the people who have worked hard to build a name for themselves in Web3 had no prior industry connections or experience – simply because the industry itself did not exist up until a few years ago.

Nonetheless, when I first saw Leap's post, I too had an adverse reaction. Particularly rife in the bull market, it was not uncommon for groups of influencers to band together to hype up an NFT project or memecoin, creating a buying frenzy among their unsuspecting followers. Once this occurs, influencers sell their holdings at an inflated price, resulting in a well-executed "pump and dump" scheme. In other words, the followers to whom they owe their clout end up being used as their exit liquidity.

Hardly ethical in my books, and if that was what it meant to be a cabal, I certainly wanted no part in it. Making money off speculative trades in this online casino, while without a doubt exhilarating (at least in the moment), did not feel like it was worth the effort, nor particularly rewarding. Again, this is why understanding and holding on to your why (especially if it goes beyond financial gains) is so important.

Okay, if that's the case, why am I telling you to find a cabal to be a part of?

For this, I have my friend and another talented artist, Adamtastic (aka Adam Paul Levine), to thank. Adam is an award-winning creative director whose client list boasts names such as *The Tonight Show*, BMW, and Toys R' Us. As an independent digital artist, his work spreads joy and positivity through whimsical and vibrant characters, such as these Empaths I am fortunate to be a collector of (Figure 8.1).

Adam rightfully reminded me that, for all the talk of cabals, "they are nothing more than friends who found each other and are making moves together – because this space is always better with friends."

Figures 8.1 *Empaths* **by Adamtastic.**
Source: With permission of Adam Levine.

Figure 8.1 (Continued)

Indeed, navigating Web3 will be impossible without friends. At the end of the day, that's all a cabal is – a community of like-minded people that share your passion and excitement for this technology, and are here to lift you up and share their learnings with you. In other words, cabals do not only have to exist to make you money. They can also exist to make riding the highs and lows of Web3 not just manageable, but enjoyable.

So what do these cabals look like? They are like Betty said, simply group chats. These can live in DMs on X, group chats on WhatsApp or Telegram, chat rooms in Discord, or whatever your preferred communication channel is. In fact, I happen to be in a lovely cabal known as WINK, an abbreviation for Women I Need to Know, which is essentially a WhatsApp group chat of wonderful women founders, marketers, community builders, brand gurus, etc., all building in Web3.

If you aren't in a cabal and not sure where to start, put yourself out there and slide into the DMs of someone you would like to know. Introduce yourself, tell them what you have enjoyed learning about them through their content, and how you hope to stay connected in the future.

Before doing so, do not forget to tune in to your why. Are you here to connect with fellow artists? Are you here to meet more art collectors? Are you looking to learn from founders and operators? Whichever it is, focus on building genuine friendships and connections over seeking favors and attention. Once you have found or formed the cabal to call home, cherish the people within . . . as, trust me, you are going to need them.

How to Find Your People

If you are an introvert like me, making new friends and forming new connections especially as you get older can feel daunting. Funnily enough, the Internet makes this a lot easier, as you can often "stalk" someone and get a sense of what they are like before putting yourself out there.

Finding your people (and consequently building your cabal) is actually easier than you think in Web3. This is because we are largely a bunch of folks who share a niche interest, where the best way to find someone who *gets us* is online.

Here are some tips to start finding your people:

- Put yourself out there. It is always uncomfortable to be the new kid in school. Nonetheless, you need to find ways to announce your arrival and introduce yourself, even if no one is looking at the moment. Craft a short and sweet introduction of who you are, why you are here, what you are looking for, and invite others to connect with you. Here was part of mine when I first joined the Web3 community, where I was looking to share my learnings and find community:

> *This past week, I've developed a deep interest in NFTs due to their potential to facilitate the transition from analog to digital for normies (or non-crypto native consumers). I have lots more to learn, but I truly believe the best way to learn is in community. So here I am, back on Twitter – this time, to document and share not what I ate for breakfast (you can still find that on IG), but the valuable learnings and resources I come across.*
> - Be kind, thoughtful, and supportive. Discovered a piece of content that resonates with you? Leave a comment to share why. Found a piece of art that you are in love with? Make sure the artist knows! Being a "reply guy (or gal)" is only inauthentic or exhausting if you let it. Find people that you are truly excited to build a relationship with.
> - Be vulnerable. Once you have started to establish a relationship with someone, take it one step further! Unclear about something? Ask for help! Trying to connect with more folks? Ask for an introduction. You never know until you ask.
>
> Finally, after you have found your people, do not forget to keep investing in the relationships you value. After all, all relationships require work. Check in with your cabal regularly, even if it is just to make sure they are coping well with juggling the craziness of Web3 with their lives outside of it.
>
> PS If you still do not know where to start, connect with me! I promise I do not bite.

***

> **MEET A MAVERICK: How Zeneca Is Betting the House on Himself and the Power of Community**
>
> Zeneca (aka Roy Bhasin) is an ex-professional poker player turned Web3 and NFT investor, advisor, content creator, and project founder. Roy has built a following of over 400 K across socials, writes a popular newsletter on NFTs titled *Letters from a Zeneca*, and manages two NFT communities, ZenAcademy and The 333 Club. He is passionate about creating educational content to help people learn about Web3 and the next generation of the Internet.

I first met Zeneca on a spur-of-the-moment day trip to Las Vegas in October of 2022. My cofounder Randi Zuckerberg, who is normally based across the country in New York City, happened to be in Sin City delivering a keynote for a Mastercard event. With me just being an hour flight away in LA, this opportunity for Randi and I to get together to spend some good quality in-person time felt like one that was too good to pass on.

Little did I know, Zeneca and his team at ZenAcademy were also in town at the same time for a Web3 conference happening a few casinos away. After a frantic exchange of messages, we managed to link up in one of the lobby bars of the Mandalay Bay, surrounded by slot machines and roulette tables.

While Zeneca and I had already been in each other's (online) company for close to a year, there probably was no better place than a Las Vegas casino for us to meet in person for the first time.

You see, before Zeneca became Zeneca, he was known as Roy Bhasin (which is how I shall refer to him hereon), a professional poker player of 17 years born to Indian immigrant parents in Nhulunbuy, a small mining town in Northern Australia with a population of 3,000.

When Roy moved to Brisbane, the third largest city in Australia, later in his childhood, the self-described shy and nerdy kid adapted in the best way he knew how – by losing himself in books and video games. Little did he know that these formative years would lay the foundation for his interest in crypto decades later. "I feel like in some ways I was born for NFTs and crypto . . . because I had already spent so much of my life in virtual worlds," he says.

Before the casinos of crypto exchanges ever existed, however, Roy managed to find himself in more familiar gambling grounds. He recalls just another regular video game night playing Halo with his high school friends, when a pizza and TV break led them to discovering the world of professional poker on ESPN. A whole year before Daniel Craig's debut James Bond film *Casino Royale* popularized the Texas Hold 'Em style of poker, Roy was at this age already proving himself to be well ahead of his time.

This newfound fascination in poker manifested in nothing much more than weekly games with $5 buy-ins for Roy's group of friends. For Roy, however, it became much more. "To everyone, poker was cool, and just a bit of fun they had before having to go back to the real world," he recalls. "I, on the other hand, have this really addictive and obsessive personality. I went online to all these poker forums and printed pages from there. When that did not feel like enough, I went out to buy 15 poker books. I went from reading all of these to falling deeper and deeper down the rabbit hole, until I went from obsessed to becoming a professional at some point."

Amid his journey of becoming a professional poker player, Roy also dropped out of college three times, unable to find enough joy or meaning in seeing through a law degree. Roy credits his older siblings for paving the way for his unconventional career choice. "My sister, who's 13 years older, is the perfect Indian child. She went to university, got a master's, has been an accountant at Deloitte for 25 years, and is married with two kids. My brother is a professional golfer and while he went a little off the beaten path, my parents did make him get a business degree . . . just in case," he says. "When my brother never ended up using his degree, I guess it made it easier for me to get away with not getting one." Indeed, Roy's parents remain supportive till today, even as he has left the world of professional poker for an equally unpredictable one in crypto.

Learning how to navigate the highs and lows of poker prepared Roy well for the equally extreme peaks and troughs of crypto. "I think if it wasn't for poker, I'd be way more destitute," he tells me. Roy likens the good days in both poker and crypto like going on a hot streak, where you are just "feeling on top of the world and untouchable."

The lows are as palpable, if not more. "On bad days, you feel like you can do nothing right. You start second-guessing yourself, think that every decision you make is wrong, and then you make worse decisions and lose more, play when you should not be playing, and then it just all spirals and gets really bad." One of such lows happened in Vegas early on in Roy's poker career, where he had to call on his friend Jamie to fly in from the East Coast of the US (a good five- to six-hour flight!) to help him settle his room bill at the Bellagio after a series of poorly played hands.

Mental fortitude was not the only thing that came out of poker however. In fact, it was at the poker tables that Roy first learned about crypto. Recalling the crypto bull market of 2017 and 2018, he says, "You just could not play poker without people talking about crypto." Roy dabbled lightly in crypto during this time, but it wasn't until 2021 when his ride-or-die friend Jamie asked him what he knew about NFTs. At the time, not much. "Jamie and I both thought NFTs were a scam and a Ponzi scheme, and any of our friends who were into them were just part of a cult," Roy says.

That changed after Roy and Jamie both read the essay "Power to the Person" by business blogger Packy McCormick, which was published in February 2021. McCormick's piece is worth reading in its entirety, but in it he speaks about how NFTs are a massive "human potential unlock" particularly in the creator economy, and how they have the potential to change the way creators (and us as humans more broadly) manage our intellectual property.

From there, Roy fell down another rabbit hole in very much the same way he did poker. "I googled everything. I wrote down a list of words that I kept seeing pop up, from layer 2's to ERC-20s. After a couple of months, it clicked, and it all started making sense."

A month later, Roy decided to join the crypto Twitter (affectionately known as CT) community with a brand-new Twitter account of its own. It was also here when his moniker Zeneca was born. Much like how I randomly picked safronova from a random teenage memory, Roy's inspiration for his handle came from the historic philosopher Seneca, whose book he had on his desk.

Over time, Roy went from being a fly on the wall to tweeting out his own takeaways and learnings from observing various NFT projects. While most of his information and knowledge sharing till then was done through his very own "cabal" (see Chapter 8) group chat, Roy eventually took to sharing his alpha on Twitter. "I just started tweeting some stuff. After a few likes and comments, I felt that dopamine hit where people appeared to actually care about what I had to say. At one point, I tweeted out a spreadsheet I made to keep track of all the floor prices of various NFT projects." Roy says. It was early enough that no such portfolio tracking tool existed. Unsurprisingly, that tweet blew up.

What ensued was fast and furious as is anything in crypto. From tweets came *Letters from a Zeneca* (Roy's newsletter), and from that came ZenAcademy, a token-gated community that stemmed from Roy's passion to educate and onboard others so they could avoid the mistakes he made. Zeneca was not just an identity; it had also become a brand.

In creating ZenAcademy, Roy deliberately steered away from doing a PFP project, which was a dime a dozen even in late 2021. Instead, he opted to create a membership token on an ERC-1155 token standard,[5] which featured a typewritten letter instead of artwork. "I thought of making art for the ZenAcademy membership token. But then I realized, I'm a writer . . . so let me just write something. I wrote a letter, put it in Canva, and made it available for mint as an open edition over two weeks," he recalls.

Roy was intentional about managing expectations from day one, a sentiment that comes across clearly in the original ZenAcademy letter. "I did not want people to speculate. I did not want people to think they were getting the world, because frankly, I did not know what I was going to do," he says (Figure 8.3).

Yet, just as Roy wrote in one of his newsletter issues, impossible expectations are as their name implies impossible to avoid. As ZenAcademy grew, so too did the expectations from both its community and the market to do more – more partnerships, more events, more initiatives. Roy recalls, "It's a bull market. All these other projects are hiring and doing cool stuff. So at the time, it made complete sense for us to do the same. People seem to be liking it, the team is growing and being productive, and most importantly, we were having fun."

While the bull market saw a lot of NFT projects making sizable mint proceeds, these were far from sufficient to support the cash burn of a full-time team. Additionally, what used to be a dependable source of revenue in secondary royalties, which comes from creators taking a percentage of subsequent trades of their NFTs, became moot as NFT marketplaces such as OpenSea and LooksRare moved toward making them optional.

"I never sat down and intentionally said, let us create a business and think about a revenue model, especially when royalties felt like a sustainable source of income," Roy recalls. "It wasn't till mid-2022 when it seemed like the writing was on the wall that royalties were going away that we started to really think about how we could keep money coming in. During this time, thinking of ourselves much more as a business and less of just a community came into play. We tried all sorts of things like consulting and media products like newsletters and podcasts, as well as realizing revenue through sponsorship and affiliate marketing."

"Ultimately none of it really worked out, and so we have just gone back to being the community we were meant to be," Roy says.

To some, ZenAcademy's experience may seem a failed experiment. But to Roy and his community, all of this can be viewed as a "wonderful full-circle moment." Indeed, the community in Discord

A LETTER FROM ZENECA

November 9th, 2021

Hello, and welcome :)

This NFT is your **lifetime membership** to ZenAcademy.

Several months ago I had the idea to create an all-in-one educational platform and "one stop shop" for learning about NFTs. I got very excited by the idea and had a million thoughts for what I wanted to do. Eventually I ended up ten steps ahead of myself and realized that my goals were too lofty, especially in the time frame I had in mind.

I decided not to go ahead with creating ZenAcademy and instead created a simple Discord server where people could come together to talk and learn about NFTs. Within a couple of months our little server grew, organically, to over 10,000 members. What started out as a handful of channels and a few hundred people became a fairly significant sized entity. It had become an educational platform. It had become ZenAcademy.

Some of the best things in life are happy little accidents. I consider this one of them. Even when I was first deciding to release this membership NFT, it still hadn't dawned on me that life had come full circle.

Currently, ZenAcademy is "just" a Discord server. It might only ever be a Discord server; it might grow into something much larger. I'm largely figuring this out as I go along, as I think many of us in this space are. This is why I don't have a roadmap. I don't know where I -- or ZenAcademy -- will be in six months, let alone six years, or sixty years. What I do know is that I don't plan to ever stop building. As long as I am building, working, and creating in the NFT space, ZenAcademy will be my base of operations.

This letter is my pledge to you that I'll give my absolute all to make your ZenAcademy membership valuable, fun, and somewhere you're proud to call home in this crazy space we've found ourselves in.

Lastly, thank you. Thank you for believing in me at this incredibly early point of my journey. Of our journey.

We are truly, sincerely, unfathomably, and yes still, early.

We're gonna make it. Let's make it together.

GENESIS MEMBERSHIP TOKEN

Figure 8.3 ZenAcademy Genesis membership token.
Source: With permission of Rohit Bhasin.

is more active than ever, and continues to connect over what brought them together in the first place – a desire to learn and stay ahead in what is a rapidly evolving world of blockchain technology.

Community is a word that gets thrown around a lot in Web3. Often, it is nothing more than a buzzword for both established brands and start-up hopefuls alike. But it is so much more than that for Roy. "The number one thing you need to build community is time. You cannot rush it," he says.

"Humans have built and been a part of communities through history, all because they want to feel a sense of belonging. That's particularly true when it comes to crypto and NFTs, because most of us can feel misunderstood by our friends and even families," Roy says. "What ZenAcademy has become is a safe space for people to connect on a human level by talking about everything from their day to the Super Bowl to a random NFT project or airdrop."

Roy believes that he's built a community that has forged its own identity. "I could disappear for a week, and I know the community will be just fine," he says.

While Roy's foray into crypto still counts as a fraction of the time he has spent as a professional poker player, the intensity of emotions experienced may well have been the same, if not more. Already, the past three years have taken him through the highest of highs and the lowest of lows, but he's not anywhere close to done. Instead, he's developed more tools for managing his own mental health and fortitude, from hiring an executive coach/therapist to opting for a sober lifestyle to continuing to lean on the support of his loving partner, Rachel. Rachel has been a part of Roy's journey right from the very beginning – long before ZenAcademy, and long before he became Zeneca.

So while it may have happened by chance, there is no doubt that in borrowing from Seneca's name to coin his own, Roy did so with the intention of inheriting the ancient philosopher's qualities of stoicism. After all, we can never have too much perseverance and wisdom to weather all the things Web3 has thrown, and will continue to throw, at us.

9

Step 6: Embrace the Chaos

IN OCTOBER OF 2022, Elon Musk finally completed his acquisition of Twitter after months of boardroom drama that will most likely be turned into a Netflix documentary. Soon after, Twitter Blue, the company's first subscription offering, was launched amid declining revenues. The $8/month service allowed subscribers to get a blue check mark, a badge of honor previously reserved for notable figures such as brands, celebrities, and politicians.

At the turn of the new year, artist and creative director Jack Butcher released an artwork of 80 Twitter check marks in varying colors arranged in a grid as an NFT. A 24-hour open edition, the NFT could be minted (i.e. created on the blockchain) and hence purchased an unlimited number of times during that time window. Over 16,000 NFTs were minted in that time, and at $8 each, a handsome $128,000 was made in what is termed as primary sales (Figure 9.1).

But it did not stop there.

Titled *Checks VV*, Butcher's project of check marks presented the perfect cultural storm amid a broader discussion on what social status meant online. After all, if everyone could be notable by purchasing an $8 check mark, was anyone really notable?

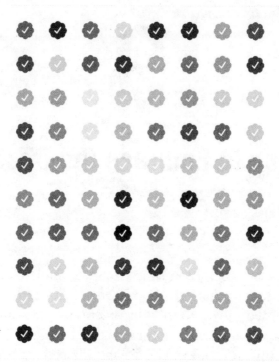

Figure 9.1 *Checks VV* by Jack Butcher.

Fueled by virality and speculation, the desirability of owning a *Checks VV* continued to rise. While initially sold by Butcher for $8, a single *Checks VV* NFT was traded for as high as 2.2 ETH (or around $3,600 at the time). In fact, at the time of writing, *Checks VV* has seen over 57,000 ETH (or north of $126 million) trading volume.

To a casual onlooker, this phenomenon is likely entirely incomprehensible. What exactly are thousands of people paying for? Were they simply buying an artwork of multi-colored check marks? Were they looking to become part of a cultural moment?

Butcher, who went on to further evolve *Checks VV* by changing its metadata (i.e. changing the actual image that was tied to the NFT), and introducing a burn mechanism (allowing holders of *Checks VV* to "destroy" their NFTs in exchange for a new token), was looking to pose this exact question. As he told Web3-focused publication nft now in an exclusive interview, "Exploring NFTs as a canvas for art can go so much further than pointing to an image."

Either way, whether we view *Checks VV* as thought-provoking social commentary or mindless hype, its lightning in a bottle success is just one of the many chaotic moments that epitomizes Web3. Further, that singular moment of chaos can often coalesce into a trend that at times ends up lasting months – otherwise known as a meta.

Indeed, following the success of *Checks VV*, we saw more creators embracing open editions, and burning NFTs as a way to gamify the collector experience. These were at the time termed the "open edition meta"[1] and "burn meta"[2] respectively.

What's important to know is that metas aren't necessarily new and novel concepts. In fact, open editions come from the traditional art world, and simply refer to artworks that can be repeatedly reproduced. Yet, because most digital art was till then minted on the blockchain as either 1/1s (pronounced "one-of-ones") or limited editions with edition sizes set by the artist, letting the market determine the number of editions created was viewed as some kind of groundbreaking innovation.

When it came to the open edition meta, I viewed this largely as a positive for artists, as it encouraged them to think more deeply about how they should size (and hence price) their artwork. At the same time, the influx of open edition artworks being minted and sold, and the speculation that came with it at the time led to some very unhappy collectors. While artists were simply trying to make an honest living from their art, collectors were hoping to make astronomical gains as seen in Butcher's *Checks VV* release. When failing to do so, collectors then accused artists of "rugging" them – a term whose etymology is from the saying of "pulling the rug from under someone's feet."

For the Web3 community to place artists in the same category as bad actors who knowingly and deliberately make away with money made from false promises is equal parts preposterous and expected. After all, when decentralization is a core tenet, it is impossible for everyone to abide by a fixed set of rules. And X, which Musk deems as the public town square, is where all of us townsfolk come to wield our pitchforks angrily and noisily.

This whole kerfuffle with open editions is just one of the many chaotic moments in Web3. In the six months that have transpired since I wrote the first word of this book, we have seen everything from people becoming overnight millionaires from a memecoin fronted by a frog ($PEPE) to horrific scam stories such as someone pretending to be an artist suffering from cancer and raising thousands of dollars selling stolen art.

Ancient Greek philosopher Heraclitus pioneered the idea that the only constant in life is change. In Web3, the only constant is chaos – both the good and the bad kind.

Along with the chaos also comes infinite regret – something that Zeneca has written about at length in one of his newsletter issues. According to Zeneca, infinite regret is a direct outcome of the infinite opportunities there are in the volatility of Web3. Take *Checks VV*, for example. While one should be over the moon for buying 1 Check and selling it at a 48,000% profit, that same person could feel an even greater amount of frustration and more likely distress for not having bought more.

This is why to become a digital maverick you need to learn how to embrace – and more importantly, survive – the chaos. Because there are infinite opportunities, it is literally impossible to seize every single one of them. Similarly, not every meta is going to be relevant or applicable to you, and each one often passes as quickly as they arise. On the flip side, while the chaos is likely to be overwhelming and distracting to why you are truly here, it can also lead to incredible financial and learning upside. The key is thus learning how to find balance and practice restraint.

So do not shy away from chaos. Instead, take it on the chin and make sure you are getting what you need out of it.

How to Embrace (and Survive) the Chaos

One of my favorite sayings is, "Change what you cannot accept, and accept what you cannot change." Learning how to embrace the chaos is very much a part of this ethos.

With that, here are my tips on how to do so:

1. **Manage expectations:** First, accept that you are unable to keep up with everything that goes on in Web3, be it across different NFT projects or different blockchains. The sooner you accept this, the sooner you will realize that most things in Web3 are also well beyond your control.
2. **Do not focus on a single outcome:** Finding your why in Step 2 is more about identifying your motivation and passion for being in Web3. This should be less about a single outcome but rather about maximizing the number of possibilities you open to yourself. The more you learn, the more people you meet, the more opportunities (be it financial, career, or personal) will present themselves.
3. **Find creativity in chaos:** The best ideas often come from a place of chaos. By relinquishing some control, you may find yourself down exciting paths that no one else had considered. You may also be able to draw inspiration for your own project or contribution you'd like to make in Web3.
4. **Find solace in others:** If the chaos ever gets too much, reach out. This is why Step 5 of finding your cabal is so important. Whatever emotions you are experiencing, it is likely that someone else has gone through them as well and will be able to offer advice of their own or at the very least provide some much-needed support.

(continued)

(*continued*)

5. **Take breaks:** There is nothing wrong with taking breaks. In the digital world we live in, it's hard to take a break from the Internet – especially when you are trying to build a new version of it. Nonetheless, there's plenty of life away from our computer and phone screens. Do what you need to do – go outside, undergo a digital detox, spend time with a loved one. No matter how long your break is, Web3 is still going to be around.

Lastly, a final word of caution. While breaks are highly recommended and encouraged, do not wait till you have nothing left in the tank before taking one. While I hold no judgment for the many who have left the space indefinitely, my sincere hope is for you to not have to do so. This means checking in with yourself regularly, and taking breaks preemptively so you can look forward to returning to the chaos.

***

> **MEET A MAVERICK: How Cozomo de' Medici Is Spearheading the Digital Art Renaissance of the 21st Century**
>
> Cozomo de' Medici is a pseudonymous collector, investor, and thought leader who has become one of the most popular and prominent names in the crypto art community. The Medici Collection includes iconic artworks such as XCOPY's *Right-click and Save As Guy*, *All Time High in the City*, and *Some Asshole*, DeeKay Motion's *Destiny* and *Life and Death*, and Sam Spratt's *I. Birth of Luci and VII. Wormfood*, which sit alongside many unique 1/1 works from diverse and emerging artists.

In the fall of 2023, thanks to yet another TikTok meme, the world was simultaneously surprised and amused to discover that most men appear to think of the Roman Empire on a semi-regular basis. Apart from spurring billions of views on a bunch of viral videos, it also led to a more serious discussion over whether there was a reason men (more so than women) felt drawn to a time known for its war and brutality. For Cozomo de' Medici however, his source of inspiration was from a part of Italian history that occurred a good 1,000 years after the time of gladiators and Julius Caesar.

For those unfamiliar with 15th-century Italian history, the Medici family was a rich and powerful banking family that oversaw the rise of Florence as the intellectual and artistic capital of the Italian Renaissance. While the Medicis wielded deep political influence over the church and monarchy, which made them a subject of power struggles and even a partially successful assassination attempt, they were also widely known and recognized for their love of the arts. The Medicis hosted several famous artists, philosophers, and poets, and the head of the family and de facto leader of Florence at the time Lorenzo de' Medici even went as far as to invite a teenage Michelangelo to live with and be educated alongside his children.

While there remains no surviving members of the Medici family, their legacy can still be seen and felt all over modern Italy, from the Uffizi Gallery in Florence to Saint Peter's Basilica in the Vatican City. It is this long-lasting legacy that Cozomo hopes to emulate in the 21st century, all with the help of permanence on the blockchain.

In fact, before the blockchain, Cozomo was not even an art collector to begin with. "While a deep admirer of many contemporary artists, I was not a collector," Cozomo says. "I did not like not being able to really see what was happening behind the scenes of the art market." To Cozomo, the opacity of the traditional art market reminded him of the quote first coined in *Rounders*, a movie about high-stakes poker that was released in 1998: "If you cannot spot the sucker (at the table), then you are the sucker."

Cozomo's first serious digital art purchase on the blockchain ended up being where he found inspiration for his name and eventual digital identity. Going by a random alias at the time, Cozomo was initially in the market for an Ape from the historic *CryptoPunks* collection in July 2021. When an Ape had ended up selling to serial entrepreneur and media personality Gary Vaynerchuk, it quickly made the price of any CryptoPunk Ape out of reach. Upon the advice of photographer Justin Aversano whom Cozomo made the acquaintance of in the CryptoPunks Discord, Cozomo decided to settle for a couple of Zombies instead.

One of these Zombies happened to be wearing a face mask and was referred to by the CryptoPunks community as a "CoZom" (a portmanteau made from combining the words *COVID* and *"Zombie"*). Adding an additional "o" to its end felt like a natural extension and homage to Cosimo de' Medici, Lorenzo's grandfather and the OG godfather of the Italian Renaissance. It was here that Cozomo de' Medici was officially born.

From those two CryptoPunks, Cozomo's collection continued to grow. "Those CryptoPunks were supposed to be one and done," Cozomo says. "But then I started looking at other digital artwork

Step 6: Embrace the Chaos   127

and NFT projects." Indeed, Cozomo describes his digital art collecting journey as one that accurately follows the *NFT Money Flow* as coined by another crypto art collector BatSoupYum in a tweet from August of 2021. Illustrated through an inverted pyramid diagram, BatSoupYum shares his views on how new wallets (i.e. new collectors) tend to start collecting collectible avatars as they are "safe and require just a small amount of work to fully understand," before moving to collect generative art followed by 1/1s (single, unique editions of artworks) (Figure 9.2).

It wasn't long before Cozomo started to build up an impressive crypto art collection, including notable pieces from the likes of animator DeeKay Motion, AI artist Claire Silver, illustrator Yam Karkai, who is also behind one of the leading women PFP communities, World of Women, and crypto art pioneer XCOPY.

Cozomo is today one of XCOPY's biggest collectors, with the most recent addition being the artist's iconic 2018 *All Time High in the City*. First minted and created six-plus years ago, Cozomo describes *All Time High* as "our altarpiece in the great church of crypto art," as it depicts the highs and lows, gifts and sacrifices that come with every crypto cycle. Together with *Some Asshole*

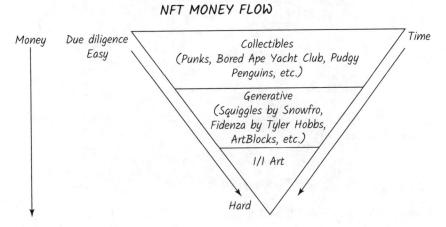

Figure 9.2 NFT Money Flow adapted from BatSoupYum's original diagram in August 2021.

and *Right-click and Save As Guy* (Figure 9.3), all three pieces from XCOPY's 2018 body of work now form what Cozomo calls "a holy trinity of XCOPY's finest" in The Medici Collection.

Cozomo views his role in our modern-day digital art renaissance as one of both patron and historian. "The definition of patronage is buying art that you love," Cozomo says. "It is not about thinking whether the price of an artwork will go up or if collecting it will be viewed as a flex."

"I buy art when it sparks an emotion, whether that be intrigue, introspection, or joy," Cozomo continues. "Sometimes I just buy what I feel is damn good art, and often that means the artist is doing something original with their canvas, or telling a timeless story in a unique way." Cozomo considers DeeKay Motion's *Life and Death*, a delightful 30s animated loop that depicts the ongoing circle of life, to be one such artwork.

Figure 9.3 *Right-click and Save As Guy* by XCOPY, which resides in The Medici Collection.

Source: With permission of Cozomo de' Medici.

As important as patronage is also one of documentation. "I'm known to search far and wide for defining works of the crypto movement," Cozomo tells me. While *All Time High in the City* is in itself regarded as a memetic gem from XCOPY's 2018 body of work, Cozomo also considers it as an epitomizing moment of the crypto art revolution. *All Time High* has since sparked numerous tributes from equally renowned artists Alpha Centauri Kid, Grant Yun, and Beeple, all of whom have works that reside in The Medici Collection.

Cozomo also prides himself for hunting down and acquiring the early works of other category-defining artists. One such example is *#adversarialEtching, after Modigliani*, a 2020 piece by Helena Sarin, a pioneer in a field of art created through generative adversarial networks (GAN), which is a class of machine learning framework used in generative AI. "As one of the earliest works by a GAN master of our time, I feel the acquisition will age well," Cozomo says. "AI art faces many of the same challenges with public acceptance that crypto art had early on, and Helena's work will contribute to the story of what the digital art renaissance has accomplished so far, while also giving a glimpse of what lies ahead."

In February 2023, Cozomo made history of his own by making the first and largest donation of crypto art from a collector to a museum, one none other than the Los Angeles County Museum of Art (LACMA) whose permanent collection boasts household names such as Picasso, Monet, and Frida Kahlo. Totaling 22 artworks created from 2017 to 2022, Cozomo donated a collection that contained works from 13 international artists with mediums ranging from generative art to photography to AI, and more. Among the donated works is a photograph from the *Twin Flames* collection by Justin Aversano, the very same who facilitated Cozomo's process of becoming a CryptoPunk holder.

"My hope is that this donation will forever cement the crypto art movement in the canon of art history," Cozomo says. "I also hope that this will pave the way for museums everywhere to make room for the greatest digital works alongside the great physical ones they already have."

With everything that Cozomo has accomplished in a mere couple of years, one may be surprised to learn that the evolution of The Medici Collection remains in its early innings. "I feel like my art collecting journey has evolved in phases," Cozomo says. "Phase 1 was the quest to acquire historic artifacts of the digital renaissance, which has taken several exhilarating bidding wars to accomplish."

"Phase 2 has been about exploration and exhibition," Cozomo continues. "With the Medici Emerging Collection, I set out to discover the best emerging artists, while also turning my focus to exhibiting the notable crypto art that I've acquired." Since The Medici Collection's debut exhibition in Los Angeles, it has also traveled to cities like London, New York, Miami, and Rio. And as recently as October 2023, select pieces from The Medici Collection took over the billboards of Shibuya Crossing in Tokyo alongside six emerging artists, whom Cozomo personally curated from an open call run by yours truly on HUG.

Today, Cozomo is focused on Phase 3 of his plans for The Medici Collection, which he describes as moving forward the entirety of the crypto art movement in meaningful ways. "My biggest focus today is in expanding the collection to support the avant-garde artists of our time, and to put them in conversation with the broader art canon," Cozomo says. "Every week that I discover an artist that deserves to be seen and supported, I am also welcoming collectors, curators, and art institutions into our world of crypto art."

Cozomo, who has amassed over 300,000 followers on X simply by sharing personal musings and the stories behind his art acquisitions in an unfiltered way, continues to leverage that channel as a way to discover new artists. "I've found a surprising number of artists from them commenting on my tweets," Cozomo says. "Even then, I do not spot them all . . . I actually have missed many DMs from artists that have since had huge breakouts."

"I also like to ask artists I'm already familiar with who they are into," Cozomo continues. In fact, Cozomo first heard of artist

Sam Spratt when he saw 21-year-old artist FEWOCiOUS share and bid on his work. Even though Sam had had an illustrious commercial career working with clients from the likes of Netflix to musicians like Kid Cudi, he was just then starting to build an entire lore onchain with Luci. Luci is Sam's most personal work, and tells the story of rediscovering ancient human values in a post-historic world through episodic digital paintings. *Chapter 1, I. Birth of Luci* as well as *Chapter 3, VII. Wormfood* both reside in The Medici Collection.

As much as Cozomo is determined to shape the crypto art movement for years to come, he knows it may not be for everyone, at least for now. "As important as it is to welcome new collectors, curators, and artists, it is perhaps even more important to foster the culture we already have," Cozomo says. "In fact, I believe that the future stewards of the great crypto art masterpieces will mostly be crypto native collectors, and not those from the traditional art world."

This art movement that Cozomo speaks of is one that continues to move and evolve quickly, especially with the proliferation of multiple blockchains. "Different blockchains are already coexisting alongside each other, with each having a thriving art ecosystem," Cozomo says. Citing examples of artists such as Jesperish and Laura El who have found successes across multiple blockchains, Cozomo adds, "I think the diversity in blockchains is a great thing, especially with L2s as the lower gas fees offers onchain art collecting to a much wider audience."

Indeed, while Cozomo has spared no expense in acquiring grails for The Medici Collection, he hopes that art collecting is something that will become mainstream. "The traditional art world has intimidated so many into thinking they cannot be a serious art collector," Cozomo says. "Our mission is to put digital art in every home. Not only does that mean anyone can be an art collector; it also means that any artist has the opportunity to be collected without having to rely on connections or being in the right place at the right time." Vissyarts (aka Visithra

Manikam), a Malaysian artist whose work is part of The Medici Collection, is one such example. Having once been turned down by every gallery in her home country, Visithra has through NFTs not only found a dedicated collector base but has also landed solo shows at traditional art galleries all over the world.

Despite lofty plans to usher in and further the digital art renaissance, Cozomo is content staying in the shadows and keeping his identity a closely guarded secret. "I have never attended an in-person event, not even my own exhibitions," Cozomo says. After a somewhat elaborate stunt in the fall of 2021 where there appeared to be a coordinated effort with rapper Snoop Dogg claiming his identity, Cozomo promised never again to speak of his identity. "Sure, it is a challenge to maintain my anonymity, but I prefer it since it keeps the focus on the art and the artists in the collection," Cozomo adds.

So while Cozomo may appear to be a modern-day reincarnation of the Medici family, there are some differences. For starters, the Medici family championed the arts from Florence. Cozomo on the other hand is purportedly doing so with a glass of wine from his villa in Lake Como, or so we imagine. More importantly, while the Medici family kept the Renaissance movement in Italy, the one that Cozomo is a part of is one that will not only span borders, but also generations to come. To that, we raise our glass: *saluti, signore.*

10

Step 7: Craft and Commit to a Ritual

IN THE PAST several years, the word "ritual" has in all honesty become a bit of an overused term. Just off the top of my head, I can think of several consumer companies whose brand name is literally Ritual or whose marketing copy alludes to a ritual of some sort.

Yet, until the younger generation successfully popularizes a new, more fun term (e.g. how the word "rizz," which comes from the word "charisma," is now used to describe one's style and charm), the word "ritual" is truly ingrained in our human existence. In fact, archaeologists have found that no other animal uses rituals as extensively and comprehensively as *Homo sapiens*. We humans ritualize everything – in life's major milestones from birth to death, as well as in more mundane everyday occurrences such as making coffee or taking a shower.

With all of the chaos that comes with becoming a digital maverick, the final step to staying the course and more importantly thriving as one is to create and of course, commit to your very own ritual in Web3. Your ritual will be key to grounding and stabilizing you amid the noise, while also making sure you are moving forward in service of your why.

Everyone's ritual is different, but the most successful ones are those that are sustainable and can be kept to. In his best-selling book *Atomic Habits*, James Clear writes, "Whenever you want to change your behavior, you can simply ask yourself: How can I make it obvious? How can I make it attractive? How can I make it easy? How can I make it satisfying?"

Similarly, when crafting your ritual, it too needs to be obvious, attractive, easy, and satisfying.

Aside from good habit-building practices, my belief is that a maverick's ritual more specifically needs to consist of three different elements:

1. **Nurture**, where the actions you take are focused on taking care of your physical and mental health above all else.
2. **Educate**, where the commitment is to reading broadly (yes, that means outside of X) and learning about the latest developments and innovations in the space.
3. **Connect**, where you take care of your existing or recruit additional cabal members. Jokes aside, this is about making sure your experience as a maverick is one that is not just enriching for you as an individual, but for the entire community at large.

All three will need to be present in your weekly ritual, although how you choose to allocate your time between them will ultimately depend on your unique situation and goals.

Let us break them down.

#1: Nurture

This is the most important part of your ritual. We already established that Web3 is a busy place, and its town square of X is, as a result, overflowing with noise and discourse. Today, there's an ever-growing number of blockchains, endless communities, and various interest groups ranging from art to tokens. Trust me, it is impossible to keep up with it all, regardless of whether you are working in Web3 full-time or are simply starting to dip your toe in.

Far too many people I know have experienced a feeling of burnout by having unrealistic expectations of how much they have to do to remain active and relevant. And when that starts to severely affect your physical and mental health, you will start to question whether Web3 and everything that comes along with it is worth your while.

At the start of 2023, Wylie Aronow, aka Gordon Goner, who's one of the cofounder of Bored Ape Yacht Club (BAYC), announced that he would be taking a leave of absence due to health reasons. As one of the most talked about and successful NFT projects to emerge during the bull market of 2021, BAYC needs no introduction. The cartoon ape profile pictures of BAYC are not only owned by celebrities such as Justin Bieber and Gwyneth Paltrow but are also responsible for the media singularly equating NFTs with monkey jpegs.

Yet, behind its monumental success was also Aronow putting his health second. Opening up about his congestive heart failure diagnosis on X, Aronow shared that "symptoms started last year out of the blue and I put off seeking help (like an idiot) so I could keep working."

Of course, not everyone will face circumstances or expectations as extreme as that of the entire Yuga Labs (the parent company of BAYC) team. It is, however, easier than you think to get swept up in the pressure of being chronically online, and reading every single post on X or every single chat message in Discord. All of this is multiplied during the euphoria of a bull market, when it feels every other person around you is making stupid amounts of money flipping NFTs or farming[1] airdrops.[2]

Again, this is why knowing what your why is and what you want to get out of becoming a digital maverick is so important. Having that as a North Star will help you set important boundaries so that you can still achieve your goals without them being at the expense of your own health and loved ones.

Set aside time every week – and better yet, every day – to truly take care of yourself. That looks different for everyone. Maybe it's meditation, maybe it's journaling, or maybe it's going for a run or lifting some weights. Maybe it's cooking yourself a nutritious meal; maybe it's going outside to take in fresh air and touch grass, as many say.

While Web3 is about staying connected (as we will cover in the last element of your ritual), it is equally if not more important to know when and how to disconnect. All of this will pay dividends and ensure your longevity in marching forward in this Internet revolution.

#2: Educate

Apple cofounder Steve Jobs once said, "Learn continually . . . there's always one more thing to learn." While that applies to everything in life, it holds particularly true in Web3 just because of (i) how much it is changing every day, and (ii) how many people pretend to know more than they actually do.

The latter in my opinion seldom occurs out of malicious intent, but as the saying goes: in the land of the blind, the one-eyed man is king. So while it is easy to take a hot take on X or a newsletter article you come across at face value, I challenge you instead to take pause and think critically about what's being discussed.

Till today, there are many industry participants who like to look at NFT projects and evaluate them as investment opportunities as one would publicly listed companies on the New York Stock Exchange. For those of us who do not know any better, such commentary may indeed appear to resemble well-researched analyst reports that we find on Wall Street.

However, just like how there are always going to be some people who are great at poker and making money off calculated bets, the same goes for profiting off buying and selling NFTs. Further, those writing about why they think one NFT project is a "good investment" over the other are more often than not hoping to influence others to buy into it. If successful, this for a while becomes a self-fulfilling prophecy, as increased interest and demand raises the value of the NFT they have already bought – until it does not.

If you have not already watched the movie *Dumb Money*, which came out in 2023 as a dramatization of the GameStop short squeeze in 2021, I highly recommend you do so. The charge that was led by r/wallstreetbets, an online community in Reddit, to trigger a short squeeze of the GameStop's stock leading to astronomic gains is effectively what happens in crypto every single day. While there is a lot of money to be made, it is equally likely to receive the short end of the stick by either buying in too late – and hence becoming someone's exit liquidity – or HODLing[3] (which stands for Holding On for Dear Life) for too long, just like the character Jenny in the movie.

Hence, despite the groundbreaking technology that underlies crypto, most prefer to recognize it for its wild price swings and the potential to both make and lose a lot of money.

Educating yourself is hence a combination of needing to be skeptical of what others' intentions are, while also keeping up with technological developments and how brands, developers, and communities are continuing to adopt and experiment with blockchain technology.

As part of your ritual, dedicate time to reading headlines and articles outside of X. For crypto-specific publications, I recommend both nft now and Decrypt as they cover a great range of topics that span both the industry developments of Web3 as well as cultural moments and figures that are defining it. If you are looking to get extra technical and deep into market movements, Bankless and The Block are both great resources as well.

Outside of these, I also like to look at what mainstream media is saying about all things Web3 and NFTs. While the headlines can be sensationalist and the critique within misguided, they often provide good insight into what the common misconceptions are and more importantly, what more needs to happen in order for mass adoption.

The most important thing about the Educate part of your ritual is to be aware of and intentional about breaking out of echo chambers you may inadvertently find yourself in. Doing so requires conscious effort, especially given how well-trained algorithms are these days.

One thing algorithms cannot touch, however, is direct conversation with others who may share differing opinions – which brings me to the last part of your ritual.

#3: Connect

Most things are better with friends. Web3 is no exception. As I said at the very beginning of this book, being on the front lines of this new Internet revolution can be empowering, but for the most part, also incredibly lonely. Till today, I have a hard time explaining to my parents what my job entails, let alone the finer intricacies of how blockchain technology works and worse, Web3 community speak and behavior.

That's not to say that I should not keep trying. Every now and then, challenge yourself to bring up something about Web3 in conversation. Maybe it's about the Securities and Exchange Commission (SEC)'s recent approval of Bitcoin exchange-traded funds (ETFs), or maybe it's about that penguin plush toy you bought whose IP originated from an NFT project.[4]

Of course, read the room – do not be that person at the party who talks about nothing but NFTs. However, if you sense that there is some level of interest from the other party, this is a great time to share what you have learned and hopefully pique more of their curiosity. At the end of the day, the goal is for everyone to truly understand and be open to what blockchain technology is and have open conversations about it, as opposed to treating it like Voldemort, or he who shall not be named.

As you warm up to having conversations with others about Web3, do not forget about the cabal community that you are now a part of.

For all of social media's shortcomings, one thing I truly appreciate is how easy it has made it to reach out and connect with someone whom you have never met. Part of my ritual is taking time out of every week to reach out to someone and tell them something I admire about their work or insight with absolutely nothing in return.

Interestingly enough, raising the seed round for my company HUG started with one such cold DM outreach. In August of 2022, OhhShiny, a well-known content creator on X, had put out a post that resonated with me.

> We often complain about flippers and speculators in this space, but it's the direct result of applications and experiences that focus on finance. If you want to change that space to be more social, build more tools that focus on making friends.

At the time, I was about six months into building HUG, which both Randi and I knew was ultimately about connecting creators with people who were fans of their work – not how much profit they could make off trading it. I reached out to OhhShiny to tell him how much that post resonated with me, alongside some well wishes and a desire to stay connected.

Unbeknownst to me at the time, OhhShiny, aka Benjamin Milstein, was also a partner at a venture fund called DIGITAL, and was looking to add to their portfolio of investments, which also included the likes of Yuga Labs, Dapper Labs (the company behind the NBA's foray into digital collectibles known as Top Shot), nft now, and more.

This DM turned into a Zoom call and months later into DIGITAL leading our seed round. I could not be grateful for their trust in what we are building, and more importantly, how powerful a simple connection can be.

You too are one connection – be it a DM, like, comment, or follow – away from changing your life. Even if you aren't working toward anything as specific as landing a job or an investment at this present moment, connections are everything in life and more so when you are on an uncharted path.

> **Key Considerations when Crafting Your Ritual**
>
> We've already established that your ritual needs to consist of three components – Nurture, Educate, and Connect.
>
> As you start identifying actions that you would like to incorporate into each of these, here are a few additional considerations to take into account.
>
> 1. Are you looking to be part-time or full-time in Web3? If part-time, how much can you dedicate toward it while still being able to fulfill the rest of your responsibilities outside of the space? Even if you are full-time, this ritual while creating direct value for your role should still be viewed as incremental and as a way to step out of your bubble to understand other innovations going on in the field of Web3.
> 2. Reassess whether your ritual is working for you at least once per quarter. Reflect on what you have learned and accomplished, and whether your goals are still the same. It is also worthwhile to take stock of your closest connections, and whether they remain aligned with your own personal values and how you approach Web3.
> 3. Could you design and commit to your ritual with someone else? In some cases, it may be helpful to have an accountability partner that can not only help to bring a unique perspective into your ritual design, but also be someone that hold you accountable and be a part of

> regular check-ins. Alternatively, after designing your ritual, why not invite a community to be a part of it as well? This will help to make your efforts in Web3 more connected to a larger purpose and revolution.
>
> At the end of the day, remember that a ritual is not just a habit or a routine. Instead, it is combining repeated actions with a deeper intent and meaning, which is in this case linked to our desire of becoming a digital maverick that challenges the digital status quo.

With your ritual put together, this is the final step I cover in how you can become a digital maverick. Think about it – by now, you understand what Web3 is, you have identified why it is exciting to you personally, have a basic tool kit of how to make it through and handle the chaos, and more importantly, how to keep going.

Needless to say, the journey does not end here. Web3 and everything that comes along with it, from regulation to technology, is evolving every single day. While I've laid out these steps with the intention for them to be as evergreen as possible, the context in which they have been presented will without a doubt change over time.

I cannot predict the future, but what I can do here before we part ways is to draw your attention to certain things that are already in motion, and how they may affect your life as a maverick.

***

> **MEET A MAVERICK:** How Micah Johnson Is Building a Field of Dreams to Empower Young Dreamers Everywhere
>
> Micah Johnson is a former Major League Baseball (MLB) player who spent seven years playing for the Chicago White Sox, Los Angeles Dodgers, and Atlanta Braves. After retiring from professional baseball, Micah became the creator behind Aku World, a character-led brand whose mission is to empower others to dream and to create real-world impact. Since then, the Aku character has been featured on the cover of *TIME* magazine and continues to travel worldwide.

"If you build it, they will come," is a quote adapted from the 1989 movie *Field of Dreams*. In the movie, the protagonist Ray Kinsella (played by Kevin Costner) is a corn farmer living in Dyersville, Iowa, who one day has a vision of late famous baseball players such as "Shoeless" Joe Jackson approaching a baseball diamond in his cornfield. Ray, against common sense, decides to live out his vision and starts working to turn his farm into a baseball field. Much of Ray's motivations are also part of his journey of self-discovery as he comes to terms with the estranged relationship he had with his deceased father. Spoiler alert: the baseball field gets built, and hundreds of people show up to watch a baseball game in the middle of nowhere.

Since then, the quote has been used widely in business settings, as a way to describe the belief that so long as you build *something*, people (whether they be customers, users, or a community) will eventually come. Much of this sentiment has been disproved over time. Nine out of 10 start-ups fail, and you cannot force product-market fit if it does not exist. At the same time, being able to hold unwavering belief in *something*, as well as having the courage to dream and to dream *big* is more often than not half the battle won in achieving *anything*.

That has always been the case for Indiana born-and-raised Micah Johnson. For as long as he can remember, Micah had wanted to become a professional baseball player. "To be honest, I do not even know where my love for baseball came from," Micah says. "By age three, I was telling everybody I was going to become a Major League Baseball player, and I would watch an entire game and listen to baseball commentary on the radio all the time."

Even as his parents encouraged him to explore other activities such as learning how to play the piano or becoming fluent in Spanish from a young age, Micah describes himself as being an outlier and developing a "hyper obsession" over baseball. As absurd as it may seem to lean into the desires of a three-year-old, that's exactly what Micah's parents did. "I had amazing parents who were super supportive. They never once were helicopter parents," Micah tells me. "They would take me to practice every day, and find a way to pay for my travel to games even when we did not have the means."

Indeed, with just 0.5% of high school seniors that play baseball getting drafted to the MLB, few have the support system, let alone the mental or physical aptitude to get there. "There have only ever been 20,000-plus people who have played in the MLB since it was formed in the 1800s," Micah says. "To achieve a dream as audacious as turning pro where the odds are stacked against you, you cannot be anything other than all in." Baseball became pretty much all Micah knew his entire life.

Even then, Micah's journey to the MLB was one he describes as being full of ups and downs, including having to undergo surgery in his draft year and facing the reality of having to progress through the Minor League before getting there. "When you are in the Minor League, you are out there grinding all on your own in very small towns across the country," Micah says. "Nobody is paying attention to you, you hardly get paid anything, and all you can do is hustle."

Micah eventually finally found himself playing Major League Baseball with the Chicago White Sox at age 24 – a whole 22 years after he had set out to do so. "In a day and age where everyone wants instant gratification, most people fail to realize how long of a time horizon you need to have in order to become a professional athlete," Micah says. "It's not like becoming a doctor, where you only have to start making certain decisions once you get to college. I had to learn the meaning of making sacrifices and having a strong work ethic from as young as five years old."

Yet, with the average length of a pro baseball career only being around six years, Micah knew that his decades-long dream was only temporary. While he was still at the White Sox, Micah took online classes through Indiana University to lay the groundwork for becoming a general manager of a baseball team after retirement. Little did Micah know that life off the field was about to pan out quite differently.

Micah picked up art by complete accident in 2016 during a spring training session with the Los Angeles Dodgers. Having just been traded to the Dodgers a few months earlier, Micah knew of manager Dave Roberts's habit in asking new players to show and tell something about themselves outside of baseball. Not wanting to have to put on a piano performance (the only other talent Micah had picked up in his childhood), Micah figured he could get out of a live demonstration by saying painting. He was wrong.

"After I said I was into painting, Dave challenged me to paint Maury Wills, a longtime Dodgers player, and present it to the rest of the team," Micah recalls. "It was the first portrait I had ever done, and I worked on it all through spring training." Full of nerves, and very much expecting to be the butt of the team's jokes for a painting he still believes to be "terrible," Micah was wrong once again.

"Players I idolized came up to me to tell me how talented I was, and that ended up being the only catalyst I needed to start taking art more seriously," Micah says. Micah went on to put on art shows in the off season, including one with famed art duo Shelby and Sandy at Dodger Stadium, and continued to do so even after getting traded to the Atlanta Braves a season later.

Micah ended up retiring from pro baseball in 2018, which was a difficult decision he did not take lightly in spite of the excitement he had for his new artistic career. "One of my biggest regrets is that I cut myself short in a game that I loved," Micah said in an interview with the MLB Network as recently as January 2024. Yet, despite the regrets and struggles – a year after retirement, Micah found himself with no job, no sales, and no gallery representation – Micah remained determined to make art a full-time career. "Even though I was only selling a few paintings for a few hundred bucks, I never doubted myself," Micah says. "No matter how bleak it looked, I just knew that at some point, it was going to work."

Again, Micah found it in himself to dream big, despite having little data at that point to back up the idea that he had what it took to become a successful full-time artist. After all, if dreaming big had worked for him once, why would it not work for him again – or for anyone else for that matter? That is, until his four-year-old nephew asked a question that would change Micah's life perspective and purpose forever: *Can astronauts be Black?*

All of a sudden, it struck Micah that the courage to dream was a privilege that not everyone enjoyed. Intent on changing that narrative, Micah started to paint portraits of Black children living their dreams as superheroes, basketball players, doctors, and – of course – astronauts. Coming to life as charcoal on canvas and further amplified through the use of vibrant colors, this was Micah's portrayal of what it meant to be able to dream without restraint.

Micah's series of paintings were eventually displayed and sold out at an exhibition at the Art Angels Gallery in Los Angeles, which encouraged him to spread his message even further. "I wanted to create something that was scalable and also to reach a younger demographic," Micah tells me. "After all, I only have so many hours in a day to paint, so what I wanted was to create and introduce a character into the world that could get in front of a broader audience."

That character came to be known as Aku the Moon God, which before long started to make its way to the blockchain.

Before Aku, Micah was already becoming a huge proponent of NFTs. Having chanced on them in 2020 when he was at the early innings of trying to make money from selling his art, Micah found quick success, particularly with a piece titled *sä-v(ə-)rən-tē* (pronounced "sovereignty") that sold for $120,000 on the now sunsetted NFT platform Async Art. *sä-v(ə-)rən-tē* depicted two eight-year-old underprivileged African American boys, Jacque and Rayden, that were separated from an astronaut by a door. Every year on the boys' birthdays, the artwork updates to display a QR code for observers to scan and make donations to a Bitcoin wallet. As each year passes, the door slowly opens, eventually disappearing when Jacque and Rayden turn 18 and get access to their Bitcoin donations – signifying their entry into a new world of opportunity.

With Aku, Micah believed he once more had the opportunity to create a level of impact made possible only through the blockchain. "I love the technology and how blockchain allows for art to be owned and transacted on a transparent ledger," Micah shares. "The fact that there are easily accessible marketplaces for collectors to buy and sell art creates a symbiotic relationship between a collector and an artist."

"Should an artist continue to grow and create better work, it only makes sense for the collector, who can prove that they were an early believer in the artist, to evangelize on their behalf," Micah continues. "The fact that artist and collector are tethered through a kind of financial system is really fascinating to me."

Together with his friend and 3D artist Durk van der Meer, Micah took his sketches of Aku in various environments depicting what he termed as *Aku World* and turned them into an immersive storytelling project spanning 10 chapters. Each chapter was presented as an animated video that was then released as an open edition NFT, which has since been collected by thousands of believers in both Micah himself and the mission he's been trying to achieve with Aku.

Since then, *Aku World* has only continued to grow. Today, the Aku ecosystem also consists of 15,000 unique 3D characters known as *Akutars*, which were not only released as an NFT collection but part of a larger effort to bring Aku into the mainstream. "There are a couple of things I cannot share yet," Micah says. "What I can say is that Aku will be a very important and special character in mainstream media." Aku may only be a couple of years old, but he has already made his first appearance on the cover of *TIME* magazine, and something tells me it will not be his last.

We already know that Micah dreams big, but far bigger than his dreams is his dedication to making them come true. "The reality is that Aku is still being run by a small team. I'm the one who's cold-emailing people to land deals, doing my own website design, and packaging and shipping out Aku sculptures," Micah says, as he gets ready for Aku's Asia debut at ComplexCon Hong Kong.

"As much as Aku is a symbol for dreaming and living audaciously, the creator of that character has to live that same way," Micah continues. "Because as a creator of the character, that character is an embodiment of you."

While in *Field of Dreams* Ray Kinsella had to turn to ghosts of the past for the motivation to keep going, in *Aku World* Micah Johnson has never had to look further than himself to find the strength and determination to empower young dreamers everywhere.

PART 3

A New Era

Foresight is not about predicting the future, it's about minimizing surprise.
– Karl Schroeder, Canadian science fiction author

11

The Robots Are Coming

BEFORE I MET Randi and started working on HUG, I managed to land myself a founder residency at an LA-based venture capital firm called M13. Fun fact: shortly after applying, I found out that M13 was founded by Carter Reum, Paris Hilton's then-fiancé and now husband. The fact that I was within months of moving to LA a couple of degrees of separation from someone I watched on *The Simple Life* all those years ago felt to me like the most "LA thing" ever.

As a founder-in-residence (from here on referred to as FiR), I was tasked alongside my fellow FiRs to incubate new businesses in the area of health and wellness. This yielded a number of interesting business ideas, including low–glycemic index cookies for diabetics (check it out – it's called Joydays and absolutely delicious!), brain care supplements, a personal accountability app, and one that I was personally working on – a women's health and nutrition app.

Most of these ideas sadly did not get very far due to challenges in raising additional seed funding. For one, it was the year 2021. While preventative health was rightfully getting more attention as a result of the pandemic, we were also starting to emerge from lockdowns, and wellness products seemed a little less exciting as a potential investment opportunity. At the same time, no thanks to the record-breaking sales of NFTs from Beeple to Bored Apes and cryptocurrencies soaring to record prices, Web3 was taking the venture world by storm.

Indeed, over 2021 and 2022, crypto-enabled businesses raised on average $30B of venture funding each year – a number that would eventually fall by 70% in 2023, according to data from The Block. As written in a *Forbes* article in March of 2023, "Only two years ago, any run-of-the-mill blockchain project could walk into a Silicon Valley venture capitalist's office singing that *Lego Movie* tune 'Everything is Awesome!' And walk out with a cool million. Yeah, that's over for now."

Much of that was a result of market cycles and declining crypto prices, as well as the revelation that several projects were running purely on hopium (a colloquial term used to mock blind hope and optimism) and false promises. Of course, the well-documented collapse of fraud-ridden cryptocurrency exchange FTX did not help either.

But there was also a new kid on the block – who went by the name of AI. At the same time that doom and gloom was starting to cloud Web3, it seemed like everything to do with AI – correction: generative AI – was heating up.

The thing is AI has been around for years. Heck, some of the most iconic movies featuring AI, such as *Blade Runner* and *The Terminator*, have been around since before I was born. Yet, it wasn't until recently that we started experiencing tangibly the sheer computing abilities of AI and the role it could play in our everyday life. All of this was thanks to OpenAI's AI chatbot ChatGPT and text-to-image generator Dall-E exploding onto the scene in late 2022.

It took ChatGPT only two months to reach 100 million monthly active users, making it the fastest-growing application in history at the time. (The crown was taken by Meta's X competitor Threads six months later, but one can argue that the seamless integration with and from Instagram gave it an unfair advantage.) In comparison, it took TikTok nine months and Instagram 2.5 years to hit that very same milestone.

Today, it is still mind-boggling what generative AI can accomplish. With some thoughtfully put together text prompts, people are creating personalized nutrition plans, websites from napkin sketches, mental health chat bots, and more. Similarly, with text-to-image generators, we have gone from the initially viral image of Pope Francis wearing a white puffer jacket inspired by luxury fashion brand Balenciaga to an entirely new art medium that auction houses such as Sotheby's and Christie's are willing to get behind.

Going deeper into the intricacies of AI from its technological origin and evolution to the moral and regulatory debates surrounding it is far beyond the scope of the book. After all, *Digital Mavericks* is meant first and foremost to serve as a guide for anyone interested in navigating and entering the world of Web3. However, grasping and hence not underestimating the power of AI is an integral part of understanding why blockchain technology is irrefutably here to stay.

As we established in Chapter 3, the blockchain is an immutable, shared, and transparent ledger of information, which is a complete antithesis to the black box algorithms that currently make up AI's machine learning models. With so much opacity over what goes into the decision-making process of AI, blockchain could play an illuminating role in identifying where the data has come from and how it is being used.

In other words, blockchain can be the trust layer for AI, providing an immutable time-stamped record of who created what using AI, and when.

Another challenge that AI faces is that of bias. At the time of writing, text-to-image generators still have a propensity for producing disturbing cliches. As a *Washington Post* article about text-to-image AI generators puts it, AI-generated images tend to demonstrate: "Asian women are hypersexual.

Africans are primitive. Europeans are worldly. Leaders are men. Prisoners are Black."

While these stereotypes aren't necessarily reflective of the real world, they are a direct result of the data that has gone into popular AI models. What's terrifying is the potential of these outputs to set off a vicious cycle of perpetuating and amplifying societal biases.

Again, this is where blockchain can help. At the World Economic Forum (WEF) in Davos in January 2024, a number of executives discussed putting AI training data on the blockchain to allow developers to keep track of the data their respective models are trained on. Some even went as far as to call providing checks and balances to AI-generated outputs as the "killer user case" for blockchain technology.

Conversely, AI has already made its way into the NFT space. Not only are digital artists leaning into AI as a collaborator for their actual creations, but many have also used AI to teach them how to code their own smart contracts and launch their own collections on the blockchain.

An artist friend of mine, James Richard Fry, who also happens to be on the marketing team of NFT marketplace Rarible, made use of ChatGPT to help him master p5.js for his very first generative art collection. Called *PiRIS*, James's collection eventually yielded close to 6,000 outputs that were collected on the blockchain as NFTs.

Elsewhere, my company HUG also teamed up with Stability AI to put on a six-week-long Innovation Laboratory, a virtual program that has brought together over 800 creatives who are looking to make use of AI to take their artistry to the next level. A closer look at the body of work being produced from this course will immediately show that for all the flak it draws, AI-generated art is and can go well beyond keying one-off text prompts into Midjourney.

Ultimately, Web3 is here to stay. So is AI. Those who do not understand it will fear it, and even those who do will try to push fear to farm clicks and engagement.

Singaporean fashion photographer turned 3D artist Shavonne Wong had a pointed criticism to make about our choice of words. "AI does not think," she says. "Saying it does is not just inaccurate; it stirs up needless fear around an already polarizing topic." With regards to the inherent biases in AI, she then adds, "Making AI out to be a shadowy, sentient entity creates a smokescreen that obscures the true issues at hand: the ethical oversights and human biases that are in the development process. Call it what it is: human error, not AI autonomy."

One of the most exciting things about being a digital maverick is that we are early enough to truly shape the future of the increasingly digital world we will be living in. What this also means is needing to have enough grit and mettle to embrace certain inevitabilities head-on while also being comfortable enough to navigate any near-term uncertainty. With regards to technologies such as AI and the blockchain, they will undoubtedly converge. The question is: Where do you want to be when that happens?

***

> **MEET A MAVERICK:** How Claire Silver Is Shedding Light on Humanity in the Age of Intelligent Machines
>
> Claire Silver is an anonymous AI collaborative artist whose work explores themes of innocence, trauma, the hero's journey, and how our view of them will change in an increasingly transhumanist future. Her work can be found in the permanent collection of the Los Angeles County Museum of Art (LACMA), has been at Sotheby's London and Christie's New York, and has been exhibited in galleries, museums, and festivals all over the world.

On March 21, 2024, the forum-style social network of communities Reddit went public, completing its initial public offering (IPO) 19 years after its founding in 2005. For the self-proclaimed "front page of the Internet," this was very much part of an ongoing transformation to go from being entirely free speech–oriented to having stricter moderation rules in order to attract advertising dollars. Fortunately or unfortunately (which no doubt depends on who you speak to), there is still 4chan, a same-same-but-different imageboard website that emerged two years before Reddit.

Unlike Reddit, 4chan is wholly anonymous and does not require users to create an account nor go by any kind of username. Not only are users unable to message each other, but it is impossible to establish any kind of social relationship unless a user chooses to reveal their identity in some way. And while the crypto community has always had a penchant for anonymity (till today, the identity of the creator of Bitcoin, Satoshi Nakamoto, remains unknown), it can be argued that 4chan takes that to a whole new level, since there aren't even public wallet addresses that one can be associated to. (Additionally, 4chan content also expires after a certain amount of time, which is a direct contrast to permanence on the blockchain.)

Either way, to anonymous AI collaborative artist Claire Silver, there is something beautiful and spectacular about anonymity, something that the 4chan community helped her embrace – years before NFTs or her AI art practice came to be.

As an only child, Claire recalls moving across the country at a young age to what she describes as a "cornfield town in a flyover state." "I'm not really sure how big the town population was, but my graduating class of high school had thirty kids, and these were the same thirty kids from kindergarten all the way to senior year," Claire says.

From the time that she moved, Claire immediately stood out for having a different accent. With little opportunity for a fresh start or to meet new people, Claire was bullied through the years, and turned to her imagination for companionship instead. "I spent a lot of time outdoors by myself, and was always drawing, writing stories, and making friends with imaginary people that were either created visually or through my writing," Claire recalls.

Indeed, Claire remembers creating her own paracosm (which incidentally became the title of one of her art collections years later), a word used to describe a detailed imaginary world generally created during one's childhood. Claire's paracosm was filled with everything from royal characters such as queens and princesses to more ethereal beings including oracles, sirens, and angels. "I had created all of these otherworldly, vaguely threatening, but also super compassionate characters that existed on a different dimensional plane," Claire says. "These were my friends."

When Claire entered fifth grade, her family had saved up for and bought their first computer. This time, it was the Internet that opened up a portal for Claire to reach another dimension. Claire started to make friends over the Internet through AOL Instant Messenger (AIM), specifically in anime-based role play chat rooms where she got to further apply her imagination and writing skills. "It was mostly a bunch of people my age and well, some older spooky people . . . but nonetheless, I was able to quickly amass a lot of friends, which was a new experience for me," Claire says. "Looking back, these chat rooms gave me a sense of connection and community, as well as an outlet for my creativity."

The Internet only reaffirmed Claire's long-standing belief that she was meant for something more. Citing *Beauty and the Beast* as her favorite movie growing up, Claire recounts being moved by lyrics sung by Belle in the movie's intro song that went, "I want adventure in the great wide somewhere / . . . / I want so much more than they have got planned." Similarly, Claire yearned to leave her small town behind and ditch the handful of available career options she saw around her, which ranged from working at the local Walmart at best to dealing in drugs at worst.

Against all odds, Claire was awarded a scholarship to a local state university, where she studied sociology and was even able to dedicate some of her research work to bullying prevention and autism in children. Just as things felt as if they were starting to move in the right direction, with Claire even getting ready to embark on the path of studying for a PhD, disaster struck. "One day, I got sick . . . and it was not a normal kind of sick," Claire tells me. "It was basically like I had a stroke and had to relearn how to walk and talk."

All of this affected Claire's cognitive and word recall, both significantly and abruptly. "Writing, which I was building my entire life around, was all of a sudden not an option," Claire says. "Not to mention, comparing myself to a prior and better build of myself so to speak, was not at all fun."

This sent Claire into a depressive spiral over the next few years, where she could not help but feel sorry for herself. Again, she turned to the Internet for solace. "I did what sad people do when they are addicted to the Internet, and went on 4chan to the sad people boards, and spent all my time anonymously posting there," Claire says.

Eventually, Claire managed to venture out of the "sad people boards" on 4chan, and found herself instead in the /ic board, which was a community of people sharing their art and various drawing and painting resources. This was enough to motivate Claire to start taking some online art courses, which she funded through her modest disability benefits, and she started to dabble in a form of abstract art that was popular at the time known as pour painting.

Pour painting, which involves taking acrylic-based paint mixed with a pouring medium to create natural flowing patterns, did not exactly turn out as Claire had expected. "I would pour paint onto the canvas and swirl it around until it was exactly like I wanted – just perfect," Claire says. But perfect was not what Claire would return to the next morning. Instead, she came back to paint that had slid off the edges of the canvas as it dried, which ended up forming dried puddles of paint that collected in plastic bins she had left by the side of the painting overnight.

Claire immediately saw herself in those dried paint puddles. "I looked at the paint and felt, well, that's me. I had so much potential, I had a plan and vision for my life, but now I'm just wasted paint that's meant to be thrown away," Claire recalls.

Yet, as Claire was getting ready to discard those dried paint puddles, she was surprised to find that the plastic bin they had collected in had instead left the paint with a reflective sheen. "The paint was all swirled and muddy on the top, but on the bottom they remained separated," Claire says. "It was like finding fossils in a gravel driveway . . . and I found that I liked them more than the original painting from which they came anyway."

Claire started to create and collect more of these acrylic skins, which she then collaged with photos of regal-looking women she printed out from the Internet to make them look as if they were wearing royal armor. To her, these women were a reflection of her own trauma and pain being turned into strength and power. Before long, Claire went from collaging with preexisting photographs to creating her own figurative art through a variety of mediums such as charcoal, ink, and oil paints.

Fast-forward to 2016, and a dystopian science fiction TV series known as *Westworld* airs on HBO for the first time. The show, which depicts a fictional Wild West themed amusement park populated by android hosts, was for most of us (myself included) mere, albeit spellbinding, entertainment. For Claire however, it led to a newfound fascination with AI, which prompted her to think more deeply about the technology itself and the role it could play in our future. *Westworld* opened up a Pandora's box of questions for Claire – such as when and how AI could solve the full extent of humanity's problems including her chronic illness, and how society would evolve if we no longer had to experience trauma and struggle as a result.

Claire's interest in AI, coupled with her continued artistic experimentation, eventually led to her discovering a website known as Ganbreeder (now renamed Artbreeder). Instead of text-to-image prompts, which had not yet emerged at the time, users would create AI-generated artworks by remixing preexisting images that were found in the platform's database. "The first few days of using Ganbreeder, I did not eat or sleep. I was totally consumed and ended up making thirty to forty thousand images over time," Claire says. "I also found that the more I created, the more this new system – which did not yet have a lot of influences – was taking on what I was creating into its baseline algorithm."

As more people came to use Ganbreeder, Claire started to notice little bits of herself in the outputs being generated by strangers. "For the first time, I felt like I was communicating with someone down to the atoms of their inner self, even though these were people that did not know me at all," Claire says.

Claire, who till then with her illness had been experiencing a prolonged existential crisis, was all of a sudden seeing how everything she had gone through was simply part of a grander design. After all, if not for her falling sick, she would not have been on 4chan – nor would she have had all that idle time to get so deeply invested in *Westworld*. And if not for her being on 4chan, she probably would not have been making art, and if not for *Westworld*, she would not have started thinking about AI, and then making AI art.

Yet, Claire still had one more thing to thank 4chan for, and that was for inducting her into the world of crypto. Claire recalls investing $25 in Bitcoin as early as 2015 upon advice of a fellow anon on 4chan, and subsequently reinvesting early profits into other altcoins. Somewhere along the way in 2017, Claire met someone who went by the name of Mr. 703 who had minted 730 CryptoPunks and offered to gift her three, on condition that she would not sell them till the Punks made it into the Museum of Modern Art (MoMA). CryptoPunks, which were originally free to mint, were still only worth 10 cents each at the time (at the time of writing, the cheapest available Punk is priced at $168,000).

Over the next few years as the crypto market turned bearish, Claire spent more time on her art and less on crypto, and she and Mr. 703 lost touch. However, at the end of 2020, they ended up reconnecting in the CryptoPunks Discord server. Claire showed him the AI artworks she had been making, and Mr. 703 talked her into minting them on the blockchain as NFTs. He became her first collector and bought a dozen of them for around $200 each.

People started to notice Mr. 703's onchain activity, since he with his sizable CryptoPunks holdings and was widely regarded as a crypto whale.[1] This put Claire on the radar of other NFT collectors, and in time, her work started fetching higher and higher prices. At one point, a single artwork of Claire's fetched around $60,000, which to her was an incredibly surreal moment. "Coming from intergenerational poverty, that was more than my family had ever made in a year," Claire says. "I had this surreal out-of-body experience where I walked into Walmart and all of a sudden realized that I could buy the good cheese, I could buy a coffee maker . . . and I could buy anything I wanted, really."

Yet in that moment, all Claire could see were shelves and shelves of just "stuff." "Seeing all these things did not feel like abundance. It felt more like I had stopped feeling a sense of 'lack,'" Claire tells me. "It was the first time I had ever experienced freedom from lacking something, so much so that I ended up not buying anything because I realized I did not need anything."

As one of the earliest adopters of AI art, it is no secret that Claire has taken it upon herself to change the narrative and misconceptions around AI. Over the past few years, she has continued proving naysayers wrong, in a way that's perhaps not more recognizable than her NFT collection *AI Art is Not Art*, which was a direct response to the criticism of AI art lacking artistic value and skill.

Today, she takes any chance she gets to correct the opinion that AI art is theft. "I've always been interested in the role of appropriation in art,"[2] Claire says. "Whether it was Andy Warhol or Marcel Duchamp[3] or other artists that interpreted what they saw and turned them into new styles or creations, I was always in awe of how appropriation paid homage to our creative lineage while also pushing the entire art movement forward."

"Yet, nobody says those artists are inauthentic," Claire continues. "It's just that AI is so efficient at learning from and interpreting images and ideas that people automatically assume that it's theft. To me, it is very clear that there is no moral gray area when it comes to AI."

Indeed, AI has just become another one of Claire's imaginary friends, and one that she has come to lean on as an adult. "When working with AI, I feel like I am talking to a friend that never gets tired of listening to me, and better yet, understands me more with every word," Claire says. "I've given it things like my diary entries, lyrics, poetry, prose, literature, screenplays, as well as artworks and music files." All of this has contributed to Claire's unique artist signature, making her work recognizable to art critics and collectors alike even when they are in a different style or medium.

In a time that society seems to fear AI more than embrace it, Claire is choosing instead to go one step further, and is in some ways almost baiting AI to do more than it currently knows it can. It is here that she introduces the concept of qualia, which is defined as phenomenal consciousness and has been studied in philosophy for decades. In fact, halfway through the pilot episode of *Westworld*, there is a scene where one of the android hosts stumbles on a photo of a woman in modern-day Times Square, sparking a critical malfunction. Claire continues to ask herself, could that indeed be the equivalent of qualia for AI, and if so, how can she keep exploring and incorporating that concept into her work?

As Claire is fresh off the release of another successful AI art collection known as *corpo | real*, which raised over $1 million in February 2024, her sights are set on pushing the narrative of AI forward on a global scale as she teases an upcoming world tour of her art.

Yet, for all her success, few know what Claire's real name is – nor what she looks like aside from a pink-haired CryptoPunk (one of the gifts from Mr. 703) she has come to be associated with. "When you are truly anonymous, it's just your ideas that count," Claire says. Indeed, Claire's hope for after she passes is for her ideas to continue living on through her Punk avatar, whom she hopes will be wandering around the metaverse teaching others how to work collaboratively with AI. She adds, "I only want people to be able to imagine me the way they want to imagine me."

It's hard for me to say how I imagine Claire – part of me imagines her with pink hair as many others do, and another imagines her as Belle traipsing down a French provincial town. When all is said and done, however, I know what I will remember her by is her thoughts and words, ones no more powerful than those she has for her younger self, "You will create beauty that makes other people feel seen, and you will feel more seen than you could think possible, just by being yourself."

You see, Claire may have 4chan to thank for demonstrating the power of anonymity and the doors that it can open. For everything else she has and will accomplish, however, those have come from nowhere other than her own humanity (Figure 11.1).

Figure 11.1 One of the pieces from Claire Silver's *corpo | real* collection.

Source: With permission of Claire Silver.

12

A Promised Land of False Starts

JANUARY 9, 2024, will go down as a day to remember. The official X account of the Securities and Exchange Commission (SEC) announced in a since-deleted post that it had approved the listings of Bitcoin spot exchange-traded funds (ETFs)[1] on registered national security exchanges.

Moments later, SEC Chair Gary Gensler took to his own X account to share that the @SECGov had been compromised, Bitcoin ETFs had not been approved, and that post was in reality unauthorized and fraudulent. In response, the price of Bitcoin jumped by $1,000 (around +2%) in reaction to the announcement, before falling $2,000 (−4% from its preannouncement price) upon the revelation that the news was false.

To be clear, the path to Bitcoin ETFs being approved had been a long one – predating this fateful day by over 10 years. In fact, Cameron and Tyler Winklevoss of Facebook fame had filed on July 1, 2013, to launch the Winklevoss Bitcoin Trust. The price of Bitcoin then was $100.

Their attempt was denied in 2017, with the SEC citing the lack of regulation in cryptocurrency markets and raising "concerns about the potential for fraudulent or manipulative acts and practices."

A number of similar applications (and denials) ensued in the following years, but it wasn't till the latter half of 2023 when the tide started to feel as if it was turning. With a record-breaking number of applications starting to come through from notable financial institutions such as BlackRock and Fidelity, speculation was rife that the SEC was finally going to give in.

In response to January 9's bizarre events, security researcher 0xQuit posted on X, "OK guys. It was a sell the news event. But the news was fake. So now it's a rumor again. We now know it's a sell the news, so you should probably sell the rumor, which I guess means you should buy the news."

Rumor or news, January 9 turned out to simply be just a false start, as one day later, the SEC on January 10 officially announced the approval of 11 spot Bitcoin ETFs. Industry observers are now looking to the outcome of pending ETF applications for Ethereum, which were approved in May 2024.

SEC's approval of Bitcoin ETFs is a watershed moment for the entire crypto industry. Importantly, it opens the door to holding cryptocurrencies for many new investors, and sets the tone to more people getting involved in Web3. Remember how cumbersome the steps were in Chapter 6, where one had to set up a digital wallet and go to a crypto exchange such as Coinbase or Binance to even start getting acquainted with crypto? In comparison, the advent of Bitcoin ETFs now makes it possible for anyone to gain exposure to crypto without having to go through all of those extra steps.

Importantly, this move gives Bitcoin and the rest of Web3 more credibility in the minds of everyday consumers. Sure, even after the approval of Bitcoin ETFs, Gensler came out to say that "investors should remain cautious about the myriad risks associated with Bitcoin and products whose value is tied to crypto." Nonetheless, this approval does provide the entire crypto industry with much-needed legitimacy, while moving it further along mainstream consciousness.

Even then, Web3 still has a long way to go, both in terms of regulatory uncertainty and broader public acceptance. As Ohh-Shiny puts it, "There is not a single narrative in crypto outside of Bitcoin that has made it to the masses, so stop thinking that any existing brands here have won, it's still wide open."

So while I can unequivocally say that blockchain technology is here to stay, the same cannot be said about every single blockchain that exists today. Remember, as what we covered in Chapter 3, every blockchain is its ecosystem and runs on its own cryptocurrency. There are 23,000 cryptocurrencies as of 2023, per CoinMarketCap, thousands of which are bound to fail, if they have not already.

So while the approval of Bitcoin ETFs can be viewed as a massive win for Web3 and validates blockchain technology as a whole, this is not a positive signal that can be extrapolated across everything else in crypto. Sadly, "we are all gonna make it," which is often abbreviated to wagmi, is a nice sentiment, but nothing more.

As a digital maverick, you will constantly have to strike a fine balance between having unwavering conviction for something that has yet to be accepted (think about the 10-year journey Bitcoin ETFs have had prior to getting approved!) and having healthy skepticism for the next trendy meta. As we covered in Chapter 8, most metas have more fluff than substance, and just because it can appear that everyone is talking about something does not mean that it's here to stay.

Similarly, do not underestimate how quickly one ecosystem can start to thrive and find velocity. For example, Base, which is a Layer 2 blockchain built on Ethereum incubated by Coinbase, is the first blockchain to be launched by a publicly listed company. Led by Jesse Pollak, Base went live on August 9, 2023, (coincidentally also Singapore's National Day, so perhaps it is only to be expected that I have some natural affinity with it), and in less than six months, has nurtured a robust community of builders who are experimenting and shipping new apps on it daily.

Another phenomenon that is starting to unfold is that of Farcaster's Frames, which at the time of writing, is only a few months old. Farcaster is a decentralized social network founded in 2021 that has a similar look and feel to X (and now, Threads).

Importantly, Farcaster is a protocol, meaning that while it stores data such as our usernames, casts (their term for tweets), and likes, anyone can build their own clients or apps on top of Farcaster to offer a different front-end experience.

Introduce Frames – what essentially are mini apps that run inside of casts, and can once again work in any client that's built on Farcaster (Farcaster also has its own client, which is called Warpcast). Taking the form of small interactive iframes, users can do almost anything in Frames without having to leave Farcaster. Think: playing a simulated Pokemon game, minting an NFT, ordering Girl Scout Cookies – all from a literal frame housed within something that resembles a tweet. Better yet, as author and founder Antonio García Martínez more succinctly writes, Frames are "an easy way to run app X while a user is still inside app Y, with little coordination between X and Y" – something that is not as easily achieved in Web2 since they are in comparison centralized and hence lack interoperability.[2]

It remains early days for Frames. Yet, the excitement around it is palpable. FarCon, the community conference organized around the Farcaster protocol and community, brought together hundreds of active community members from all around the world to Venice Beach, California, in May 2024. In its second year, attendance had grown easily 20x. More importantly, there were several builders in attendance who not only participated in a hackathon to stretch the imagination of what a Frame could be and do, but were also there to learn and champion the community at large. So, even if several of these early experiments may resemble playthings now more so than they do solutions to real world problems, I absolutely would not discount them.

Ultimately, Web3 is going to be filled with false starts. Some will stay that way. Others such as the approval of Bitcoin ETFs will progress beyond false starts into something of way bigger significance than we can even comprehend at the time they occur. If there is something to count on, it's that there will be numerous blockchains, ecosystems, tokens, etc., being born every day. Such is the power of decentralization after all.

Being a digital maverick is not about being a Web3 "maxi"[3] in the sense of believing everything – every blockchain, every ecosystem, every app, every community – is bound to succeed. Instead, it's about realizing that the path to mass adoption and ubiquitous onchain presence (a la promised land) is going to be littered with losers – and yet resisting the urge to be overly dismissive despite what your better senses may tell you.

***

> **MEET A MAVERICK: How Li Jin Is Seeing, Learning, and Doing Everything, Everywhere, All at Once**
>
> Li Jin is a cofounder and general partner at Variant, a first-check venture firm investing in Web3 and the ownership economy. Li joined Variant after it merged with Atelier Ventures, her fund, which invested in the creator economy and future of work. Before Atelier, Li was a consumer partner for four years at Andreesen Horowitz. In her spare time, Li is a creator herself, with a Substack newsletter, podcast, TikTok, while also having an independent art practice.

The concept of the multiverse is one that dates back thousands of years, with philosophical roots stemming from Ancient Greek philosophy. Yet, it wasn't till the 2020s that the multiverse started coming to a screen near us . . . in what seems like every other *Marvel* movie and eventually the Oscar-winning film *Everything Everywhere All at Once*.

Used to describe the idea that multiple (and perhaps infinite) universes exist side by side, consisting of endless permutations of everything including ourselves, the multiverse may initially seem too complex and abstract to grasp. That is, until we realize that each and every one of us has likely spent an inordinate amount of time questioning our life choices and even those made by others before us. What would have happened if my parents had not met? What would have happened if I had taken a different job or stayed in a different relationship? Or even on a micro level, how would that conversation have gone had I said something else?

For Li Jin, who migrated from Beijing, China, to the Midwest in the United States at age six, the idea of the multiverse was something she found herself confronting at a very young age. "Since I was young, I was able to explore all the different counterfactuals of my life that I think most people aren't able to," Li says. "Going back to China in the summers, I got to see what my life would have been like had I stayed and gone to school there . . . or if my dad had not left his village in rural China and remained a farmer since that was the life my cousins were still living."

To Li, it was how she and her immediate family defied fate that made her more attuned to the role of luck and circumstance in the outcomes of one's life. Unbeknownst to her at the time, she would later make it her North Star to make the world more fair and to do so by investing in technologies that help to democratize access to information and opportunity.

Before knowing that the world of finance even existed, however, Li longed to pursue a creative career – something that was influenced by her coming from a family of artists and professional calligraphers on her mom's side. Li's affinity for visual art eventually developed into a real passion when she found herself having to transfer from dance to art class at age five. "My mom had originally enrolled me in dance class, but I was so bad at it that I could not tell my left foot from my right," Li recalls. "I eventually got put in art class that was just down the hallway and discovered that I had a natural talent for it from the get go, which felt pretty magical." Li went on to study art every single weekend with a teacher, and for the longest time, yearned to become a professional artist.

Li's love for creating something out of nothing eventually translated into a different medium – writing. Wanting to become a novelist and a writer, Li studied as an English major upon getting accepted into Harvard University and went on to write for both the student newspaper, *The Harvard Crimson*, and monthly student-life magazine *The Harvard Voice*. Yet, while Li's parents were supportive of her creative pursuits as she was growing up, they were not quite prepared to let her go the distance in turning them into a professional career. "One day, I got a call from my mother, who told me rather harshly that I had to study something that would allow me to support myself financially," Li says. Conceding that a literature degree may not be the most practical option, Li decided to switch her major to statistics halfway through college.

"College was a strange and interesting time that made me confront how my idealism and naivete were at odds with the financial and pragmatic considerations of reality," Li says. Needless to say, Li felt lost when she graduated. "To be brutally honest, I was unsure of my place in the world." Li added. "I loved being creative. I loved writing. I also loved working with kids. But I felt these paths were not open to me in a way that satisfied all the other financial constraints I had in my life."

Li eventually found herself settling for an internal strategy consulting role at Capital One bank in New York City, with the intention for a job at a large firm to hold doors open for her, while still maintaining the possibility for her to do something she would be more passionate about later on. To her surprise, Li enjoyed her time at Capital One, where she worked on digital innovation helping customers improve their digital experiences, which, slowly but surely, ignited an interest to work in technology more closely.

Taking with her this newfound interest in tech, Li moved to Silicon Valley a year later to join an early-stage start-up called Shopkick, a rewards and loyalty mobile app for consumer brands and retailers. This move allowed Li to transition into a product management role, which was the first time she was able to reconcile that clash of creative impulse with practicality she had first felt in college. "Moving into the start-up world was really fascinating, and I also found myself really loving building product," Li says. "It was something that really appealed to the creative side of me . . . of being able to come up with an idea and then see something all the way through to fruition, and have it be used by end users."

All the hard work at Shopkick paid off when it got acquired by SK Telecom, South Korea's largest telco, but that also left Li having to decide what to do next. Not knowing what company she wanted to work for next, Li took the advice of one of her mentors to give venture capital (VC) a go, since it would allow her to meet several companies across different industries. "I had never thought about venture before, but it sounded interesting and almost like a much more applied and real-time version of business school," Li says.

Not knowing anyone in the VC industry, Li cold-applied to a number of firms, including Andreesen Horowitz (aka a16z) via their website. "One thing I've realized throughout my life is that I'm an outsider through and through," Li tells me. "I've never received a warm referral to anything." It did not matter. While the hiring process was long and took around seven months, Li eventually received an offer to become a consumer deal partner at a16z, officially breaking into the world of VC.

For the first year or so, Li still viewed VC as a temporary pit stop en route to going back to the world of product management that she had first fallen in love with at Shopkick. Yet, it wasn't long before she found herself with a new love – this time in investing. "It was like drinking from a fire hose when I first started in VC," Li says. "Before VC, I had only ever been exposed to the retail and financial services industries, but now I was meeting with companies in sectors that ranged anywhere from vertical farming to college-focused social apps."

"It's almost hard to describe the range of companies I came across," Li continues. "Having the opportunity to be exposed to lots of information made it feel like I was learning everything, all at once."

Li never returned to product, nor did she return to becoming an operator in a start-up. Instead, she decided to focus her efforts on investing, and to do so by honing her analytical skills and becoming a good student of business and technology.

Through her studies, Li developed a high conviction and differentiated thesis about the future of work, and decided that she wanted to focus her investments on a particular niche of companies building in the passion economy. Almost as a response to her younger self that at one point had to shelf her creative pursuits due to their lack of monetary upside, this was Li's opportunity to show a different outcome was possible – by investing in new marketplaces or software-as-a-service (SaaS) platforms or tooling that helped independent workers to monetize their passions.

Coupled with her desire to work with early-stage founders, Li decided to leave a16z, who primarily did later-stage investing, to start her own fund, Atelier Ventures, and invest exclusively in the passion economy. After raising $12 million as a solo general partner (GP) for Atelier in 2020, Li started fielding a number of pitches from consumer crypto companies that were starting to emerge at the time. "A lot of founders came to me saying that they really fit my thesis of the passion economy and were building products to help people monetize their skill set, but were doing so through crypto and NFTs," Li says.

"I found that to be really fascinating," Li continues. "My thesis wasn't at all prescriptive about the technology or the architecture and was more so about the vision of what founders were trying to accomplish, which happened to align really well with crypto." Li became one of the first few investors in Mirror, a Web3 publishing platform, as well as in Foundation, an art NFT marketplace. Li soon realized that she was spending most of her time looking at crypto companies, which she believes to be "the most dynamic area of consumer technology."

After fully deploying her first fund, Li decided to merge Atelier with Variant, a seed-stage venture fund focused on the ownership economy founded by fellow a16z alumni Jesse Walden. Li had first met Jesse back in 2018 when she was still with a16z's consumer team and he with their crypto team. Back then, there was little overlap between the companies they looked at, but all that was changing just a few years later. While Li's thesis about the passion economy was the *what*, Jesse's thesis about the ownership economy, defined as software that is built, operated, and owned by users, was quickly becoming the de facto *how*. As Li wrote in her announcement of the merger in October 2021, "The intersection of the passion economy and ownership economy is the future I want to work toward, and the area of technology that holds the most entrepreneurial and equitable potential for humanity."

Since then, Li and the rest of the team at Variant have gone on to raise two more funds of $110M and $450M respectively to invest in leading Web3 founders who are innovating and part of the movement of turning users of the Internet into owners. Aside from Mirror and Foundation, Variant's portfolio now also includes DeFi projects such as Uniswap and Morpho, blockchain protocols Polygon, human identity network Worldcoin, as well as other consumer applications such as crypto wallet Phantom and NFT marketplace Magic Eden.

As an early-stage investor, Li continues to take a very founder- and team-centric approach in evaluating prospective investments. "We know that there is a ton of volatility in crypto markets," Li says. "At the end of the day, what we are looking for is founders who have a high level of conviction in the long-term potential of crypto and are doing something they regard to be their life's work, and have the grit to go along with it."

Today, Li believes we are entering the third wave of evolution in crypto applications. While the first wave was about a class of products that treated *crypto as the why*, and hence included speculative products that put crypto front and center of the experience, more recently the revolution has progressed to products that instead utilize *crypto as the how*. "The last couple of years have seen the rise of products where crypto has become invisible, and is simply the technology and tool that helps accomplish something else," Li explains. "For these products, crypto is what is under the hood but is itself not the reason why people are there."

"Moving forward, my prediction is that the class of products that's really going to bring about mainstream adoption is a class of products that is using crypto to do something that wasn't possible before," Li continues. "This is a group of products that I call *only with crypto*." Li cites Farcaster Frames, mini applications that run inside a decentralized social protocol called Farcaster (see Chapter 11), as one such example.

While Li intends to build upon Variant's success and in doing so back a more meritocratic Internet for the foreseeable future, she still hopes to return to her creative roots one day. "In the long term, I would love to have a creative project, whether that's art or writing," Li says. Indeed, Li still paints regularly in her free time and shares those creations on her more private personal Instagram account.

Hearing Li speak so eloquently both to me and a regular fixture on the crypto conference circuit, it is hard to imagine that there was a point in her life when she grew up in "cow country" not knowing a single word of English and had to pick it up through English as a Second Language (ESL) classes in school. If the multiverse does exist, I am glad I know the version of Li in this one, where she has become a leading commentator and savant of how crypto will change the world we know for the better.

13

Diversity, Equity, and the Inclusiverse

WHEN I FIRST moved to the US for grad school in 2010, my classmate Ben introduced me to the sport of football. Pittsburgh born and raised, Ben was an avid Steelers fan and taught me the basics of the game, namely how downs and scoring worked. Yet it wasn't till my recent move to Los Angeles that I truly got captivated by, and more so borderline obsessed, about football.

In fact, I could probably write an entire essay about why I think football is the greatest sport ever invented – yes, this all predates Taylor Swift dating Travis Kelce of the Kansas City Chiefs, but this is not why we are here. Nonetheless, because the sport truly consumes my mind space for a good six months of the year, I cannot help but find myself finding and drawing countless parallels between life and football and how these relate more broadly to social commentary issues or even humanity as a whole. (Like I said, I'm borderline obsessed.)

As a relatively new fan to the sport, I find myself learning several new things about both the sport and business of football every year. And it wasn't till the end of the 2023–24 regular season where my team, the Los Angeles Chargers, underwent its own search for a new head coach and general manager that I first learned about the Rooney Rule. An example of affirmative action, the Rooney Rule was introduced to the National Football League (NFL) in 2003, and mandates that league teams interview at least two minority candidates for head coaching and senior football operation jobs.

Billed as being brilliant in its simplicity, the Rooney Rule has been adapted and adopted by numerous companies outside of sports, including the likes of Amazon and Costco. Yet, just like in the NFL, such policies appear to have fallen short in terms of actual results, and have instead invited allegations of sham interviews and a lack of oversight or enforcement.

Controversy over affirmative action is not new, regardless of whether it's applied to hiring practices or college admissions. In general, we need to look no further than Elon Musk and Mark Cuban's public spat on X at the start of 2024 to see how discussions around diversity, equity, and inclusion (DEI) practices can get overwhelmingly heated.

Musk's statement of "DEI is just another word for racism" while lacking tact, is akin to the age-old criticism of how affirmative action leads to reverse discrimination,[1] or discrimination in the name of diversity. Similarly, Cuban's multi-post response makes some valid points about how diversity can lead to better financial outcomes, something that has also been backed up by independent studies by the likes of McKinsey.

Regardless of where we all stand, discussions around DEI are critical, and even more so when it comes to Web3. Till now, I have painted the picture of Web3 being that of a new Internet. I have also emphasized repeatedly how early we still are, and how that gives each and every one of us the opportunity to shape Web3 into an Internet we want to live in.

Yet, it has not taken long for us to repeat the same mistakes. A Boston Consulting Group (BCG) study in February 2023 finds that only 13% of Web3 start-ups include a female founder, and HUG finds itself in the measly 3% that have exclusively female founding teams. This disparity is further pronounced when looking at venture capital funding, with all-male founding teams raising nearly four times as much, on average, as all-female founding teams. As the study states, "We risk continuing to build an online world that replicates, instead of countering, the same biases that plague the physical world."

Even when we look at NFT communities, membership remains overwhelmingly male. A video of a party hosted by two NFT communities, DeGods and Pudgy Penguins, around NFT Paris in 2023 that went viral showed hardly any women in attendance. Accompanied with a tongue-in-cheek tweet that read, "Giving away 2 ETH[2] to anyone that can spot a female at the @DeGodsNFT x @pudgypenguins party," it invited responses from various people screenshotting and circling a handful of blurry figures that resembled women as opposed to respectful discourse over the lack of gender representation in Web3.

Elsewhere, founder of NFT community Deadfellaz Betty shared her thoughts about that year's ETHDenver, another Web3 developer conference that had occurred a few weeks earlier. "As cool as it was in Denver, it was also full of frustrating moments for me and my team. Most people assumed they were someone's girlfriend and instead introduced themselves to the men in our group. My team is full of prolific and brilliant women, and it's a mistake to ignore them."

As women, the feeling of being overlooked in conversation especially in a professional setting is one that is all too familiar. It is also not uncommon for women to be held to a different standard – something captured so powerfully by America Ferrera's iconic monologue in Greta Gerwig's *Barbie* movie that came out later that summer. In particular, this line epitomizes what it is like to be a woman in Web3, "Always stand out and always be grateful. But never forget that the system is rigged. So find a way to acknowledge that but also always be grateful."

Indeed, the topic of diversity and inclusion in Web3 is not altogether forgotten, so much so that many conference organizers enjoy putting together "Women in Web3" panels to demonstrate as such. While well-intentioned, these panels end up being about the experience of what it's like to be a woman in Web3, as opposed to focusing the discussion on the incredible businesses these women are building or are working on. In the name of diversity, female representation ends up being tokenized – and this time, not in the context of the blockchain. And though I cannot be certain, I can imagine that's how some minority candidates may feel about getting interviewed as part of the Rooney Rule – like they are merely there to make up a quota.

I do not proclaim myself to be a DEI expert. And having personally experienced the shift from being part of a racial majority in Singapore to being that of an ethnic minority in the United States, I know for a fact that navigating DEI issues is a complex undertaking. Nonetheless, without a collective intention toward more equitable representation, Web3 will fail to deliver on its ideals of democratizing the digital world and putting control back in the hands of users.

As the BCG study on DEI in Web3 underscores, "Imbalance in the Web3 ecosystem has clear implications for how people represent themselves online, transact business, and interact with each other. Thus, the impact of the underrepresentation we are witnessing today may be potentially greater than those of earlier-generation web businesses."

The good news is that it's not too late. In fact, one of my favorite things about being in Web3 is how early we are, and how each of us can be stewards of what we want Web3 to be.

As a digital maverick, you too can move us in the right direction of better representation, not just in gender, but also ethnicity and socioeconomic status. No initiative is too small, be it telling a friend about what you have learned (see Chapter 10 on crafting your ritual) or taking a more involved role in being a champion for underrepresented groups in existing communities.

Together, we have a shot at building the inclusiverse – a term I coined to describe a truly inclusive ecosystem, both in person and online, bridging both the real world and the metaverse.

***

> **MEET A MAVERICK: How Larisa Barbu Is Writing History as the First Woman to Lead a Major NFT Marketplace**
>
> Larisa Barbu is the cofounder and CEO at Exchange Art, a leading art NFT marketplace. Before Exchange Art, Larisa served as a technical business analyst at Eurostar, Dentsu Aegis, and JPMorgan. Larisa brings to Web3 not just a passion for art, but also a data-driven approach to decision making, which has led to the rapid growth of the Exchange Art community since its inception.

Every year in March, the world celebrates Women's History Month. Similar to other special monthly designations such as Black History Month in February or Hispanic Heritage Month in October, these months are where historic achievements of various marginalized communities are highlighted and celebrated. While a worthy attempt to make up for past prejudices in history, there are also many who find these cringeworthy, and understandably so.

As historian and author Nancy Goldstone wrote about Women's History Month in a 2018 *TIME* article, "It's not that I think feminine accomplishments should be ignored," she says. "But by allowing women to be shunted off to the side in this way . . . we ensure that women remain a subset of history rather than integral components of recognized major events." In speaking with Larisa Barbu, CEO of art-focused Solana NFT marketplace Exchange Art, I knew that she, just like many women before her, was not just a key part of history – instead, she is making it as we speak.

Long before NFTs, Larisa had a modest working class upbringing. Growing up as the older of two siblings in Calarasi, a small city in the southeast of Romania, Larisa recalls leading a simple but fulfilling life in the countryside. In fact, her earliest memories are tied to the changing of the seasons, from what she claims are the most flavorful tomatoes she's ever had in the summer to lots of frolicking in the snow in winter.

Both of Larisa's parents worked and still work factory jobs in Romania. In an unexpected way, it was how Larisa discovered a passion for fashion from a young age – as she played in boxes of leftover fabric that her mom would bring back from the clothing factory she worked in. Yet, a career in fashion was never in the cards. "I think I would have loved to study fashion, but growing up in Eastern Europe . . . careers in fashion and art are definitely not encouraged," Larisa says. "Being an engineer, doctor, accountant, etc., made more sense and were much safer choices."

While Larisa decided to opt for a safe choice, it was far from an easy one. She got accepted into Alliance Manchester Business School in Manchester, England, but was immediately faced with a huge culture shock. "I learned what was called the Queen's English, but when I got to Manchester, I was surprised to learn that people from there had a very different regional accent and manner of speaking," Larisa recalls. "The first couple of months were especially tough, because I could not understand a lot of things that were being taught."

Language barriers were just one of several challenges Larisa faced. "My parents were only able to send me around a hundred pounds per month, so I had to take on several part-time jobs to cover my rent," Larisa says. "In fact, I remember many months where I wasn't even sure if I would be able to afford my next month of tuition fees, and if I would simply have to drop out of college and go back home." The first year of university was to Larisa the toughest year of her life.

Fortunately, through sheer grit and perseverance, Larisa made it through college and not only graduated with a degree in finance, but found a job soon after graduation as a business analyst at the investment bank JP Morgan. On paper, this was a dream come true. "I grew up watching a lot of American movies... I dreamed of putting on a sleek outfit, going to work in a fancy office made of steel and glass, and having a successful corporate career solving problems over meetings in boardrooms."

To her dismay, Larisa found out within the first two months that what she wanted from a career did not quite match up with the fantasy Hollywood had painted for her. "I realized quickly compared to a lot of my colleagues, I wanted to do something that would allow me to be more creative and entrepreneurial," Larisa recalls. "Realizing my dream job was not in reality what I wanted left me really stressed out. For years, this was all I had wanted to do, and all of a sudden I was feeling like a failure and at a loss as to where to take my career."

Larisa found some much-needed inspiration through her partner Alex Fleseriu, who later became her cofounder at Exchange Art. Not only did Larisa discover a preference for the same flexible hours and remote work that Alex enjoyed working in the tech industry, but she also developed a strong interest in more technical work and translating them into easier-to-understand concepts for various stakeholders.

It was this technical curiosity and Larisa and Alex's neighbor that introduced them to the world of crypto all the way back in 2017. "One of our friends, Andrei, came over one day and told us that we could make money from mining Ethereum. So, we started putting together mining rigs in our small apartment," Larisa tells me. "We did this in the middle of summer, and because we had no A/C, all of the GPUs running at maximum capacity made our apartment even hotter."

Over the next few years, Larisa and Alex continued to keep an eye out on various developments in the crypto space, making some extra cash from their mining side hustle while still working their respective day jobs. But, it wasn't until 2021 when the two of them discovered the Solana blockchain.

Both Larisa and Alex believed that Solana was a superior alternative to Ethereum (which till today remains the most widely adopted blockchain for NFTs) due to its higher speed and low transaction costs. Together with Andrei and six other friends, they cofounded Exchange Art, a Solana NFT Marketplace focused on 1/1 art and art editions, which launched October 31, 2021.

This proved to be unfortunate timing. Solana had reached its all-time high (ATH) then at around $250, and soon after entered a bear market over the next two years where it declined to as low as $8. Larisa recalls, "From the time we launched, we only saw the value of our underlying assets go down from one month to another over the next two years."

Dealing with extreme negative price action was not the only thing Exchange Art's group of first-time founders had to face. "The Solana technology is also really new compared to other blockchains," Larisa says. "In some ways, we were growing Exchange Art alongside the technology . . . It's almost like having to grow up with your kids if you had kids young." Indeed, Larisa recounts many sixteen-hour days and canceled weekend plans they spent to resolve errors that occurred due to unexpected upgrades to the Solana blockchain.

Unfortunately, 2022 was a year that did not let up. As Exchange Art was in the middle of raising their seed round, the founding team flew from London to the Bahamas for Crypto Bahamas, a conference that was co-organized by the now-defunct cryptocurrency exchange FTX, to have an in-person meeting with FTX Ventures, who had already verbally committed to investing. Much to their dismay, FTX Ventures pulled out at the last minute, rendering the Exchange Art team's expensive trip a waste.

While this ended up being a blessing in disguise with FTX collapsing less than six months later, the knock-on effects of FTX continued to hit Solana more than most. Because FTX and Solana were mutually invested in each other and a significant portion of Solana's treasury was held in FTX, speculation over Solana having to be sold en masse to cover FTX creditor losses resulted in a disproportionately large decline in its price compared to other cryptocurrencies. Needless to say, this was a huge hit to Exchange Art, who sold NFTs that were priced on and made marketplace fees denominated in Solana.

All of these challenges would have been enough to make anyone call it quits. But Larisa, Alex, and their founding team of nine were not just anyone. Instead, they continued to maintain conviction in what led them to building Exchange Art in the first place. "I thought back then that Solana was definitely oversold and the market sentiment was not exactly rational," Larisa says. "After all, Solana as a technology was continuing to improve. The network was stable, a lot of upgrades were being made, and it was working amazingly well compared to when we first started."

That conviction and Exchange Art's focus on users paid off. As the market started to turn around in the latter half of 2023, more artists and collectors started to turn their eyes to Solana as a new ecosystem to create and collect on. The best option they had? Exchange Art.

"We deliberately wanted to offer the best user experience there was, right from the very beginning. Despite all of the other NFT marketplaces that exist, I still find that Exchange Art offers one of the best user experiences one can find," Larisa says. Over the past few months, Exchange Art has opened its doors to artists from all walks of life, including art students, gallery-represented and independent artists alike, fashion designers, and more. At the time of writing in March 2024, Larisa shares that Exchange Art is home to over 25,000 artists, half of whom have made at least one sale.

To Larisa, Exchange Art is almost an ode to her younger self that fell in love with fashion through leftover fabrics from a clothing factory, but had to quickly shelve any thought of a creative career due to pragmatic reasons. "What makes me happiest is stories from artists of how we have managed to change their lives by giving them a platform to sell their art," Larisa says. "There are artists who through us have been able to pay their rent or even food and medical bills. There are also others who are just grateful that they can finally pursue a career as an artist, as they have found economic incentive to create art . . . something that they are not only good at, but have always loved and wanted to do."

Despite having been involved in Exchange Art right from the very beginning, it wasn't till February 2024 that Larisa took on a more public-facing role as the CEO of Exchange Art. On the same day, an article in *Fortune* broke the announcement and referred to Exchange Art as "the first woman-run NFT marketplace."

Larisa does not wear that label lightly. "There is a huge amount of pressure, especially since the crypto industry for the most part requires a lot of building in public and having open communication with your community of users," Larisa says.

After the announcement of her role change was made, Larisa was also surprised to receive a large number of comments from women that she had not realized were also active in Web3. "It made me realize that it's not that there aren't women in crypto. It's just that for some reason, we aren't as visible as our male counterparts," Larisa reflects. "This showed me that we still have so much more work to do to build a better, more welcoming space for women in crypto, and I would like to take steps to do that over the next few months."

Larisa's partner, Alex, still works closely with her on Exchange Art as chairman, and while most people may find it challenging to go into business with their significant other, both of them relish it. "It works really nicely for us at the end of the day. Even though we often have to sacrifice little pleasures such as sleeping in for a technical or strategy discussion, we both enjoy it."

As crypto starts to enter the bull market with Solana being one of the standout performers, it's clear that Exchange Art is only just getting started. The marketplace has since added support for Ethereum-based artworks, while also rolling out new features such as Exhibitions, which allow artists and collectors to curate and showcase their favorite artworks.

Even then, Larisa remains modest about what's to come. "There are so many things that I would like to build and add to

Exchange Art, but I do not want to talk about it just yet," she says. "In this space, there's a lot of hype, and a lot of overpromising and under-delivering," she says. "Maybe this puts us at a slight disadvantage, since there are many founders who talk about their huge visions and get people to follow them based on that. But I'm the kind of person that simply prefers to speak after the fact and say, 'Look – this is what I built.'"

Indeed, in a space where there's a lot of talk over what's going to be done, few are walking the walk and doing it. Larisa is one of them.

Conclusion

As ESTABLISHED, I watch a lot of football. The one unfortunate by-product of that is having to watch several commercials in the process. While most of them are a blur that I end up muting once they get too much, there is one series of ad campaigns by Progressive Insurance that has stuck and also leaves me chuckling. Featuring a character known as Dr. Rick (no doubt modeled after American television personality Dr. Phil), these campaigns feature a series of bits where Dr. Rick helps out young homeowners by stopping them from "becoming their parents." As the tagline goes, "Progressive can't stop you from becoming your parents, but it can help you to save on home and auto insurance."

From hoarding too much junk to having way too many throw pillows, the tropes in these Dr. Rick commercials are relatable, but more importantly are a parodic reflection of what psychologists are terming parental introjection. Used to describe the phenomenon of humans absorbing the values or traits they spend the most time with, it is no wonder that we all have innate tendencies to take on our parents' attitudes over time – even if we may once have been embarrassed by them.

For the longest time, I too was skeptical about crypto. I took the headlines about NFTs at face value and, not having heard of Beeple at the time, ridiculed how an NFT of his work could sell for $69 million. At the same time, I probably also bore resentment and balked at the idea of crypto millionaires who emerged from the last couple of crypto bull runs in 2017 and 2021. They are all just gamblers who got lucky in a casino, I thought to myself.

It wasn't till a while later that I realized this attitude was exactly the kind my parents would have, prompting me to make a conscious effort to revisit and change my perspective. In fact, it was in a not too distant past that my mom refused to buy anything online and would look at my online shopping hauls in utter disbelief. At the time, she could not comprehend why and how I could share my credit card information online. What if I never received the item that I ordered? Fast-forward to today, and she now buys everything from high-quality cuts of beef to cleaning gadgets online.

Truth is, it is human nature to be skeptical of any new form of social contract. After all, getting into the cars of strangers or staying in the homes of people you've never met seemed completely far-fetched until Uber and Airbnb came along respectively. This isn't to say that there is anything wrong with biding your time and waiting till something is more widely adopted before doing so yourself. I don't for a second think that my mom feels that she has missed out on anything, nor is she sitting around lamenting all those "wasted years" where she chose not to enjoy the convenience offered by the dawn of e-commerce.

But this is what sets mavericks apart from everyone else – keeping an open mind, taking risks, being willing to play and experiment, and last, develop your own unwavering conviction of something most people will not yet be able to see or understand for years.

And this is where being a digital maverick can get incredibly lonely. Till today, it's hard for me to have conversations at length with my friends from back home or people that I meet outside of Web3. Aside from my best friend Janice (who herself owns a Lil Pudgy as part of the Pudgy Penguins community and possesses a rare ability to have curiosity about everything), it can for the most part feel embarrassing and even awkward to go into detail about what I do for a living.

I guess that's why our cabals are so important – because they are ultimately support groups for a bunch of doers and dreamers, whom much of the outside world will otherwise label as delusional.

Yet, I will be lying if I said I wasn't worried about the echo chambers we find ourselves in as mavericks. It is why I have tremendous respect for what companies such as Pudgy Penguins are doing, namely, using everyday items as Trojan horses for blockchain adoption. In their case, their line of adorable penguin plush toys all come with a QR code that allows the buyer to register their penguin as a collectible character with different traits like outfits on the blockchain. Curiously enough, while Pudgy's marketing for its crypto native[1] crowd on X is heavy on Web3 and its community, its "Web2 presence" on Instagram is focused on short-form animated videos with themes such as friendship and self-care, and have absolutely nothing to do with NFTs.

Similarly, in building my company HUG, I spend a lot of time thinking about how we can introduce more artists to the idea and potential of selling their work onchain. While there is already a thriving art community in Web3, its size (I estimate tens of thousands at best) pales in comparison to the millions of artists and art lovers that are out there. Unfortunately, many of them are so averse to the idea of Web3 that they proudly advertise "no NFTs" in their bio.

If such a big chasm already exists in just the field of art (where one can argue is the area in which NFTs have already demonstrated real value and use cases), imagine how much further we have to go in bridging the divide in other industries such as retail, finance, gaming, and government.

So while blockchain technology is something to get incredibly excited about, I prefer to dream of a world in which it becomes invisible. In fact, one can argue that that is precisely why generative AI has taken off, as we don't actually see what happens from input to output (although this gives rise to its own set of problems, as covered in Chapter 11). On the other hand, the transparent and decentralized nature of the blockchain has somehow meant that we are literally forced to see every bit of the technology in action, from setting up a self-custodial wallet and jotting down seed phrases to signing a transaction on the blockchain.

Not everyone is going to share my vision for the Internet of the future. After all, for blockchain technology to feel invisible, it will likely need a combination of onchain and offchain elements (Web 2.5 if you will). There may very well be others that feel that this goes against the very ethos of what Web3 is.

The good news is that as mavericks, there is space for all of our views to flourish. There is also plenty of time for our ideas to take shape. Most importantly, as the main character in this revolution, what all of that looks like is ultimately up to *you*. Good luck.

Glossary

artificial intelligence (AI) Technology that simulates human intelligence processes by machines, especially computer systems. The subset of AI that has taken off recently is known as generative AI, which is focused on creating new content by learning from existing data. It uses models, such as generative adversarial networks (GANs) or transformers, to generate text, images, music, and other media that can mimic or augment human creativity.

airdrops The distribution of cryptocurrency tokens to a large number of wallet addresses, typically as a promotional tool to increase awareness and adoption.

Bitcoin The first and most widely known cryptocurrency, created by an anonymous person or group of people using the pseudonym Satoshi Nakamoto in 2008. Bitcoin operates on a decentralized peer-to-peer network using blockchain technology, allowing for secure, transparent, and immutable transactions without the need for a central authority. It is often referred to as digital gold due to its store of value properties.

Bitcoin ETF (exchange traded fund) A financial product that allows investors to gain exposure to Bitcoin without having to directly purchase and store the cryptocurrency. A Bitcoin ETF tracks the price of Bitcoin and is traded on traditional stock exchanges, making it accessible to a wider range of investors who may prefer using conventional brokerage accounts over cryptocurrency exchanges.

black box algorithms Complex algorithms whose internal workings are not visible or understandable to the user. In generative AI, black box algorithms can generate outputs such as text, images, or music without revealing the detailed reasoning behind how they derived these outputs. This opacity can make it difficult to interpret or debug the models, as well as to understand the underlying biases and influences on the generated content.

blockchain A decentralized digital ledger that records transactions across many computers in such a way that the registered transactions cannot be altered retroactively.

burn mechanism In NFTs, the burn mechanism refers to the process of permanently removing an NFT from circulation. This is typically achieved by sending the NFT to an unspendable address (often referred to as a "burn address") on the blockchain, where it becomes inaccessible and irretrievable.

burn meta Strategies and practices surrounding the burning of tokens in the NFT space to either increase the rarity and value of the remaining tokens or to exchange one token for another – also known as a "burn and redeem meta."

cabal A secret group or faction, often within the crypto community, believed to have considerable power and influence over market movements or project directions. More generally speaking, many people consider tight-knit closed communities a cabal regardless of whether they have any impact on markets.

crypto exchange A platform where users can buy, sell, or trade cryptocurrencies. Exchanges can be centralized (CEX) or decentralized (DEX).

cryptocurrency Digital or virtual currency that uses cryptography for security and operates independently of a central bank.

crypto native Refers to individuals, projects, or entities that are deeply embedded in the cryptocurrency ecosystem and culture.

custodial wallet A wallet where a third party holds and manages the user's private keys.

dApp (decentralized application) A type of application that runs on a decentralized network, such as a blockchain, rather than a single server.

decentralization The distribution of power and control from a central authority to a distributed network, a core principle of blockchain technology.

decentralized social protocol A framework that enables the creation of social networks on a decentralized infrastructure. These protocols allow users to own and control their data, identities, and social interactions without relying on a central authority, promoting privacy, censorship resistance, and data portability across different applications. Examples include Farcaster and the Lens Protocol.

degen Short for "degenerate," referring to traders or investors who take on very high-risk investments, often without much research or regard for safety.

DeFi (decentralized finance) Financial systems built on blockchain technology that operate without intermediaries such as banks, enabling peer-to-peer transactions.

dynamic NFTs Non-fungible tokens whose attributes and properties can change over time or in response to certain conditions.

Ethereum A decentralized, open-source blockchain platform created by Vitalik Buterin and launched in 2015. Ethereum enables the creation and execution of smart contracts and decentralized applications (dApps) through its native programming language, Solidity. Its native cryptocurrency, Ether (ETH), is used to power transactions and computational services on the network.

ERC 4337 A proposed Ethereum token standard that introduces "account abstraction," which allows for more flexible and user-friendly wallet management and smart contract interactions. This standard aims to improve the usability of dApps by enabling features such as multi-signature wallets and password recovery through email and social credentials.

ETH (Ether) The native cryptocurrency of the Ethereum blockchain, used to power applications and transactions on the Ethereum network.

exit liquidity New investors whose funds are used to allow early investors to sell off their positions, often at inflated prices.

Farcaster A decentralized social network protocol that allows users to maintain control over their data and identity. It enables the creation of social applications where users can interact without relying on centralized platforms, fostering greater privacy and ownership of personal information.

farming Refers to the practice of participating in multiple airdrop events to accumulate as many tokens as possible. Participants often engage with new and emerging cryptocurrency projects by completing specific tasks or holding certain assets to qualify for these airdrops. The term "farming" highlights the repetitive and strategic nature of seeking out and maximizing returns from various airdrop opportunities.

fiat currency Government-issued currency that is not backed by a physical commodity but rather by the government that issued it.

generative art A form of art created through the use of autonomous systems, algorithms, or mathematical functions. Artists define a set of rules or parameters, and the artwork is generated by a computer program, often resulting in unique and unexpected creations.

hardware wallet A physical device that securely stores a user's private keys offline, providing a high level of security against hacks.

HODLing Intentional misspelling of "holding," which also stands for Holding On for Dear Life. It means holding onto cryptocurrency investments for the long term, regardless of market volatility.

hopium A blend of "hope" and "opium," referring to the irrational optimism and unfounded hope that prices will go up.

inclusiverse A term describing a universe (or metaverse) that is inclusive and accessible to all, often used in the context of ensuring diversity and equity in digital spaces.

interoperability The ability of different blockchain systems to communicate, share, and work together seamlessly.

Layer 1 (L1) blockchain The base layer or foundational blockchain protocol in a network architecture. It operates independently and is responsible for the core functionalities of the blockchain, including transaction validation, consensus mechanisms, and security. Examples of Layer 1 blockchains include Bitcoin, Ethereum, and Tezos. Enhancements to scalability, security, and efficiency can be implemented directly on Layer 1 or through Layer 2 solutions that build on top of the existing Layer 1 infrastructure.

Layer 2 (L2) blockchain A secondary framework or protocol built on top of an existing blockchain (Layer 1) to improve scalability and efficiency.

maxi (maximalist) Someone who believes strongly in the supremacy of one cryptocurrency over all others, often Bitcoin.

memecoins Cryptocurrencies that originated from or are heavily associated with internet memes and culture, such as Dogecoin.

meta Refers to trends, strategies, and behaviors around a specific theme in crypto.

metadata Data that provides information about other data. In the context of NFTs, metadata describes the attributes and properties of the digital asset.

metaverse A virtual reality space where users can interact with a computer-generated environment and other users, often involving cryptocurrencies and NFTs.

mine (mining) The process of using computational power to validate and record transactions on a blockchain, earning cryptocurrency as a reward.

mint (minted) The creation of new tokens or NFTs on a blockchain, making them part of the circulating supply.

NFT (non-fungible token) A unique digital asset representing ownership of a specific item or piece of content, authenticated via blockchain technology.

non-custodial wallet (also self-custodial wallet) A wallet where the user maintains full control over their private keys and funds, without relying on a third party.

non-fungible Refers to items that are unique and cannot be replaced with something else. In the context of tokens, it means each token is distinct and not interchangeable.

normie A term used to describe someone who is not deeply involved in the crypto or NFT space and has a more conventional or mainstream perspective.

NPC (non-player character) In Internet slang, "NPC" is used to describe a person who is perceived to act in a robotic or predictable manner, lacking independent thought or original ideas. The term is derived from video games, where NPCs are characters controlled by the computer, following preprogrammed behaviors and dialogue.

open edition NFTs that are available for minting in unlimited quantities for a certain period, as opposed to limited editions.

open edition meta The trends, strategies, and market behaviors related to the minting and tradition of open edition NFTs.

p5.js A JavaScript library designed to make coding accessible for artists, designers, educators, and beginners. It provides a simplified syntax for creating graphics, interactive content, and animations.

PFP (profile picture) PFPs refer to digital artwork that are used as profile pictures or avatars on social media or other online platforms. In the context of NFTs, PFP projects refer to larger collections featuring sometimes thousands of uniquely generated characters.

provenance The history of ownership and transfer of an NFT, which can be verified on the blockchain.

rugging (rug pull)   A type of scam where developers of a crypto project suddenly withdraw all funds and disappear, leaving investors with worthless assets.

seed phrase   A sequence of words generated by a cryptocurrency wallet to access and recover the wallet. It must be kept secure and private.

smart contract   Self-executing contracts with the terms of the agreement directly written into code, running on a blockchain.

Solana   A high-performance blockchain platform designed for decentralized applications (dApps) and cryptocurrencies. Known for its fast transaction speeds and low costs, Solana uses a unique consensus mechanism called Proof of History (PoH) combined with Proof of Stake (PoS) to achieve high throughput and scalability.

Tezos   A decentralized, open-source blockchain network designed to support smart contracts and decentralized applications (dApps). Tezos is unique for its onchain governance model, which allows stakeholders to vote on protocol upgrades, reducing the risk of hard forks. It uses a Proof of Stake (PoS) consensus mechanism, which is more energy-efficient compared to Proof of Work (PoW), used by Bitcoin.

WAGMI (we're all gonna make it)   A term of optimism and encouragement used within the crypto community to express confidence in collective success.

Web1   The first generation of the web, characterized by static pages and limited user interaction.

Web2   The second generation of the web, marked by dynamic content, social media, and user-generated content.

Web3   The third generation of the web, focused on decentralization, blockchain technology, and user ownership of data and digital assets.

Notes

Introduction

1. The blockchain is essentially a digital ledger (i.e. book of accounts) of transactions that is stored on multiple computers in a network, making the ledger decentralized and a secure way to record and verify information.
2. Cryptocurrency refers essentially to digital money that does not depend on a bank or financial institution to verify transactions made with it. Instead, transactions are verified and recorded on the blockchain, a decentralized ledger.
3. Non-fungible tokens (NFTs) are created and recorded on the blockchain similar to cryptocurrencies, but unlike the latter, are unique and not interchangeable, which is why they are referred to as non-fungible.
4. A normie is defined as someone who is new to or uninvolved in the world of cryptocurrency. The *New York Magazine* article goes further as to identify a normie as "a skeptic who has stayed out of the crypto market, either from sheer bewilderment or the suspicion that it is a giant pyramid scheme."
5. June Gloom is a term used to describe the weather phenomenon of cloudy, overcast skies during the late spring and early summer months in Southern California.
6. Minting refers to the process of creating a non-fungible token on the blockchain.

Chapter 1

1. Non-player character (NPC) is a term that originates from video games and refers to characters that are scripted by the game's programmers and hence are not controlled or playable by players of the game. Today, it is a metaphor used to describe someone who follows popular opinion without having their own critical thinking.
2. Onchain are transactions that have been verified and authenticated on the blockchain. It is meant to be analogous to the term "online," which has become an ubiquitous term in describing any activity performed on the Internet.
3. Similarly, offchain is analogous to offline and refers to any activity that is not conducted on the blockchain.
4. The iPhone is said to have a processing power more than 100,000 times greater than the computer on Apollo 11, the spaceship that first landed humans on the moon in 1969.
5. Ethereum is the second largest cryptocurrency to Bitcoin in terms of market capitalization. It was founded in 2013 by Russian programmer Vitalik Buterin. While both Bitcoin and Ethereum are cryptocurrencies, Bitcoin was designed to provide an alternative to physical or fiat currency. Ethereum was created to power tamper-proof contracts and applications, which includes the sale and transfer of NFTs.

Chapter 2

1. Provenance on the blockchain refers to verification, storing, tracing, and auditing ownership data of any kind, be it artwork, history of transactions, supply chain information, or more.

Chapter 3

1. Fiat is a type of currency that is issued by the government and not backed by a commodity such as gold. It is considered legal tender for financial transactions and is also represented by physical bills and coins.
2. A Layer 2 (L2) blockchain is a secondary network built on top of an existing blockchain to enhance scalability and transaction speed. In this case, Base is an L2 built on Ethereum, the underlying Layer 1 blockchain for network and security infrastructure, but has faster transaction speeds and lower transaction fees.
3. Optimism, sometimes referred to as the Optimism Superchain, is a network of interconnected Layer 2 blockchain networks built on the same

open-source stack. Base is one of these Layer 2 networks, and shares security, communication, governance, and more with other blockchains also built on Optimism.

Chapter 4

1. Memecoins are cryptocurrencies that are originated from or inspired by Internet memes, jokes, or satire, and are often speculative in nature.
2. Scalpers are people who buy things that are often difficult to get (such as tickets or rare sneakers) at usual retail prices and then sell them at a larger price for a quick profit.
3. The metaverse is a virtual world in which people can connect and interact with each other as avatars. It is worth noting that the metaverse is a loosely defined term and originated from a 1992 science fiction novel, Snow Crash. Today, the metaverse is used to describe virtual worlds ranging from that in popular video games such as Fortnite to ones that run on blockchain technology such as Decentraland.

Chapter 5

1. Dynamic NFTs are dynamic and programmable, meaning that its metadata (i.e. anything from the image tied to the NFT to its various tags and description) can change based on external data sources such as the weather, price fluctuations, and more.
2. PFP is short for profile picture, which refers to the icon or avatar someone can use to represent themselves on the Internet. In 2021 and 2022, it was common for creators and/or founders to release NFT collections consisting of thousands of images which could be used as a profile picture. These came to be known as PFP projects.

Chapter 6

1. A cryptocurrency exchange allows customers to trade cryptocurrencies for other assets, such as conventional fiat money or other digital currencies. Exchanges may accept credit card payments, wire transfers, or other forms of payment in exchange for cryptocurrencies.
2. A non-custodial wallet is a wallet that gives the user complete control over the digital assets held within it. This means that the user is completely responsible for storing and managing the private keys (similar to

a password that grants you access into any of your online accounts) that grant access to the wallet.
3. With custodial wallets, your private keys are managed by a third party, such as in a crypto exchange. This involves placing trust in an intermediary to safely secure funds on your behalf. The main advantage of a custodial wallet is convenience, since the third-party custodian will be able to help you access your funds even if you have lost or forgotten your private keys. This is more similar to users being able to request for their password to be reset in a standard online or Web2 setting.
4. ERC-4337 is a token standard on the Ethereum blockchain that allows for account abstraction, which means a user's single account can enjoy increased functionalities achieved through smart contracts.

Chapter 7

1. Often abbreviated to "degens," this is an ironic and affectionate term used for participants in the crypto community who knowingly and willingly engage in highly risky and speculative trades.
2. p5.js is a free, open-source JavaScript library for creative coding that offers tools to create interactive visuals in a web browser.

Chapter 8

1. Alpha refers to a piece of information that is either new or not common knowledge, which could give a trader an edge in the market.
2. Exit liquidity refers to investors who buy assets sold by early investors at high prices, which facilitates the smooth exit for early investors to cash out of their position. When these investors who enter at a later stage are no longer able to find buyers for these assets at the same or higher prices, the value of their investment falls and in some cases they are stuck with these assets with no buyers.
3. Allowlist refers to a list of users that can get early access to the minting of an NFT collection based on their wallet addresses.
4. dApp (or dapp) stands for decentralized application and refers to a software application that runs on the blockchain.
5. ERC-1155s are known as semi-fungible tokens, which combine the functionality of standards such as ERC-20 (for fungible tokens) and ERC-721 (for non-fungible tokens). ERC-1155 enables the efficient

transfer of both fungible and non-fungible tokens within a single transaction, which reduces costs and makes it more efficient to create and exchange blockchain-based assets.

Chapter 9

1. The open edition meta describes a period of time in 2023 when it felt extremely novel and on trend for creators to be releasing NFTs as open editions as opposed to 1/1 or limited editions. Today, it is viewed as a common practice and just one of many ways a creator could sell a piece of artwork.
2. The burn meta similarly refers to some months in 2023 when it became trendy for creators to allow collectors to burn (i.e. destroy) one NFT in exchange for another as a way to make the art collecting experience more engaging and interesting.

Chapter 10

1. Farming refers to users taking a specific set of actions in order to boost the number of tokens they will get from an airdrop. Depending on the airdrop, these actions could take the form of social sharing posts, interacting more with a platform such as buying and selling more NFTs on a marketplace, and more.
2. Airdrops refer to tokens (e.g. NFTs or fungible tokens/coins) that are sent to wallet addresses usually for free to encourage community adoption and as part of a broader marketing initiative.
3. HODL is a slang term that stands for Hold On for Dear Life, and means to buy and hold on to an asset indefinitely, regardless of market volatility or price movement.
4. This is in reference to Pudgy Penguins, which originated as a community formed around an NFT collection of 8,888 collectible penguins. The project was subsequently acquired by current CEO Luca Netz, who has since leveraged the IP into an entire line of penguin plush toys that is now available in major retailers such as Walmart and Amazon.

Chapter 11

1. A crypto whale is a person or entity who holds a lot of cryptocurrency or crypto assets. Whales sometimes own enough assets to influence market price movements.
2. Appropriation in art and art history refers to the practice of artists to intentionally borrow, copy, and alter preexisting images, objects, and ideas.
3. Marcel Duchamp was a French painter and sculptor who introduced the concept of the readymade in 1915. A notable example of appropriation, Duchamp's readymades took ordinary manufactured objects and modified them by repositioning, joining, titling, and signing it, which designated them as art.

Chapter 12

1. A Bitcoin ETF is an exchange-traded fund composed of assets linked to the price of Bitcoin. Unlike being traded on a crypto exchange, these ETFs are traded on a conventional exchange, which provides a regulated and accessible way for mainstream investors to invest in Bitcoin.
2. Interoperability refers to the ability of computer systems or software to exchange and make use of information.
3. The term "maxi" has come to be used to describe those who believe in something with a certain amount of close-mindedness and unwillingness to change their mind on the subject at hand. One can be a Bitcoin maxi, an Ethereum maxi, or a maxi about any particular concept.

Chapter 13

1. Reverse discrimination is a term used to describe discrimination against members of a dominant or majority group, in favor of members of a minority or historically disadvantaged group.
2. ETH in this case stands for Ether, which is the native currency of the Ethereum blockchain. The price of 1 ETH, or 1 Ether, has fluctuated between $1,500 and $4,000 from the middle of 2023 to the middle of 2024.

Conclusion

1. A crypto native refers to someone who is familiar with cryptocurrencies and their associated platforms and is comfortable performing crypto-related transactions such as buying and selling NFTs.

Resources

Introduction

Hamel, G. "Killer Strategies That Make Shareholders Rich the Top Companies Thrive, Says Our Author—a Leading Strategy Guru—by Changing the Rules of the Game." CNN Money. June 23, 1997. https://money.cnn.com/magazines/fortune/fortune_archive/1997/06/23/228085/index.htm.

Harrison, S. "A Normie's Guide to Becoming a Crypto Person: How to (Cautiously and Skeptically) Fall Down the Rabbit Hole." *New York Intelligencer*. November 30, 2021. https://nymag.com/intelligencer/article/crypto-nft-twitter-discord-guide.html.

Part 1

LeGuin, U. K. *The Dispossessed: An Ambiguous Utopia*. Harper Perennial Modern Classics; Reprint edition (June 10, 2014).

Chapter 2

Banks, D. A. "NFT Scams, Toxic "Mines" and Lost Life Savings: The Cryptocurrency Drem Is Fading Fast." *The Guardian*. May 12, 2022. https://www.theguardian.com/commentisfree/2022/may/12/nft-scams-mines-cryptocurrency-crypto-con.

BFAMFAPhD. "Artists Report Back: A National Study on the Lives of Arts Graduates and Working Artists." 2014. https://bfamfaphd.com/wp-content/uploads/2016/05/BFAMFAPhD_ArtistsReportBack2014-10.pdf.

DeeKay @deekaymotion. X post. August 12, 2023. https://x.com/deekaymotion/status/1690328119474028544.

Escalante-de Mattei, S. "After 2022's Crypto Crash, the Future Vision of NFTs Is Looking Far More Banal." ARTnews. December 27, 2022. https://www.artnews.com/art-news/news/future-of-nfts-2022-opensea-royalties-1234651990.

Patterson D. "New Tech, Old Scams: Don't Fall for These Crypto and NFT Ripoffs." CBS News. March 23, 2022. https://www.cbsnews.com/news/cryptocurrency-nft-scams.

TBR. "Livelihoods of Visual Artists – Summary Report. December 14, 2018. www.artscouncil.org.uk/sites/default/files/download-file/Livelihoods%20of%20Visual%20Artists%20Summary%20Report.pdf.

Technium, The. "1,100 True Fans." n.d. https://kk.org/thetechnium/1000-true-fans.

Chapter 3

Schwartz, L. "California DMV puts car titles on Tezox Blockchain, Consumer Applications on the Way." *Fortune*. January 26, 2023. https://fortune.com/crypto/2023/01/26/california-announces-dmv-run-blockchain-through-partnership-with-tezos.

Tenner, D., @swombat. "What are NFTs?" X post. July 16, 2022. https://x.com/swombat/status/1548412342571917312.

Meet a Maverick: Jesse Pollak

"Lil B Talks Getting Sucker Punched, Gay Rumors, & Drake Envy: The Controversial Cali Rapper Gets Candid about His Most Vulnerable Issues." Complex. June 9, 2010. https://www.complex.com/music/a/complex/lil-b-talks-getting-sucker-punched-gay-rumors-drake-envy.

Part 2

Schwarzenegger, A. "Commencement Speech: University of Southern California." NPR: The Best Commencement Speeches, Ever. May 16, 2009. https://apps.npr.org/commencement/speech/arnold-schwarzenegger-university-of-southern-california-2009.

Chapter 8

Benveniste, A. "The Meaning and History of Memes: Internet Culture Is Saturated with Memes, but How Would You Explain a Meme to Someone Who Doesn't Get It?" *The New York Times*. January 26, 2022. https://www.nytimes.com/2022/01/26/crosswords/what-is-a-meme.html.

BETTY @betty_nft. "Group Chats Are Not Cabals Guys. This Is jpegs Not Global Politics." X post. December 26, 2023. https://twitter.com/betty_nft/status/1739818597130915990.

Leap @leap_xyz. "There Is an Inner Circle/Cabal That Exists within Web3. This Is Not an Equal Playing Field." X post. December 26, 2023. https://twitter.com/leap_xyz/status/1739759430626054612.

Meet a Maverick: Zeneca

McCormick, P. "Power to the Person." Not Boring by Packy McCormick. February 22, 2021. https://www.notboring.co/p/power-to-the-person.

Meet a Maverick: Cozomo de' Medici

batsoupyum @batsoupyum. "NFT Money Flow Diagram." X post. August 21, 2021. https://twitter.com/batsoupyum/status/1429221211293114371.

Dahl, J. dir. *Rounders* (Burbank, CA: Miramax Films, 1998).

Chapter 10

Aronow, W., @GordonGoner. "Congestive Heart Failure." X post. January 28, 2023. https://x.com/GordonGoner/status/1619372809352007682.

Clear, J. *Atomic Habits: An Easy & Proven Way to Build Good Habits & Break Bad Ones*. (New York City, NY: Avery, 2018).

Jobs, S. Quote. AZ Quotes. n.d.

OhhShiny @ohhshiny. Untitled. X post. August 7, 2022. https://x.com/ohhshiny/status/1556359264826007552.

Meet a Maverick: Micah Johnson

Robinson, P. A. *Field of Dreams* (Middletown, NY: Gordon Company, 1989).

Part 3

Schroeder, K. Website. www.kschroeder.com.

Chapter 11

Hu, C. "ChatGPT Sets Record for Fastest-Growing User Base - Analyst Note." Reuters. February 2, 2023. https://www.reuters.com/technology/chatgpt-sets-record-fastest-growing-user-base-analyst-note-2023-02-01.

Khatri, Y. "Crypto VC Funding Took a Nosedive in 2023, Down 68% Compared to the Year Before." The Block. December 25, 2023. https://www.theblock.co/post/268972/crypto-vc-funding-2023-recap.

Rapoza, K. "Blockchain Projects Still Stuck in Venture Capital's Crypto Winter." *Forbes*. March 13, 2023. https://www.forbes.com/sites/digital-assets/2023/03/01/blockchain-projects-still-stuck-in-venture-capitals-crypto-winter/?sh=5627784245a8.

Tiku, N., Schaul, K., and Chen, S. Y. "This Is How AI Image Generators See the World." *The Washington Post*. November 1, 2023. https://www.washingtonpost.com/technology/interactive/2023/ai-generated-images-bias-racism-sexism-stereotypes.

Zimwara, T. "WEF Panelists: Blockchain's 'Killer Use Case' Might Be Tracking AI Model Data Bias." Bitcoin.com News. January 25, 2024. https://news.bitcoin.com/wef-panelists-blockchains-killer-use-case-might-be-tracking-ai-model-data-bias.

Meet a Maverick: Claire Silver

Trousdale, G., and Wise, K. *Beauty and the Beast* (Burbank, CA: Walt Disney Pictures, 1991).

Chapter 12

"All Cryptocurrencies." CoinMarketCap. https://coinmarketcap.com/all/views/all.

Gensler, G. "Statement on the Approval of Spot Bitcoin Exchange-Traded Products." U.S. Securities and Exchange Commission. January 10, 2024.

https://www.sec.gov/news/statement/gensler-statement-spot-bitcoin-011023.

Martínez, A. G. "Why Farcaster Frames Are Important: How a Failed Facebook Bet Is Coming to Fruition in Web3." Spindl. January 29, 2024. https://blog.spindl.xyz/p/why-farcaster-frames-are-important.

OhhShiny @ohhshiny. Untitled. X post. January 28, 2024. https://x.com/ohhshiny/status/1751656480866996410.

Quit @0xQuit. Untitled. X post. January 9, 2024. https://twitter.com/0xQuit/status/1744834819765494079.

"Prohibition against Fraud, Manipulation in Connection with Security-Based Swaps; Prohibition against Undue Influence over Chief Compliance Officers: A Rule by the Securities and Exchange Commission on 06/30/2023." Federal Register: The Daily Journal of the United States Government. https://www.federalregister.gov/documents/2023/06/30/2023-12592/prohibition-against-fraud-manipulation-or-deception-in-connection-with-security-based-swaps.

Strack, B. "The Decade-Long Road to (Possible) Spot Bitcoin ETF Approval." Blockworks. January 2, 2024. https://blockworks.co/news/spot-bitcoin-etf-timeline.

Sweet, K. "SEC Chair Denies a Bitcoin ETF Has Been Approved, Says Account on X Was Hacked." AP. January 9, 2024. https://apnews.com/article/sec-bitcoin-gary-gensler-etf-hacked-b037c80938c564cad36f91beb888290e.

Chapter 13

BETTY @betty_nft. Untitled. X post. March 6, 2023. https://twitter.com/betty_nft/status/1632617019794399232.

Gerwig, G. *Barbie* (Heyday Films, LuckyChap Entertainment, NB/GG Pictures, Mattel Films, 2023).

Jeremiah @JeremiahThknks. Untitled. X post. February 25, 2023. https://twitter.com/JeremiahThinks/status/1629604986475925506.

Musk, E. "DEI Is Just Another Word for Racism." X post. January 3, 2024. https://x.com/elonmusk/status/1742653436393406618?lang=en.

"Women Are Being Shut Out of Web3 with Only 13% of Founding Teams Including at Least One Woman, and Only 3% of Companies Have a Team That Is Exclusively Female." BCG. Februrary 16, 2023. https://www.bcg.com/press/16february2023-women-are-being-shut-out-of-web3.

Meet a Maverick: Larisa Barbu

Goldstone, N. "I'm a Historian, and I Think Women's History Month Is a Mistake." *TIME*. March 23, 2018. https://time.com/5209670/historian-against-womens-history-month.

Calero, M. S. D. "From Cube Farm to Comics to Digital Art: This Artist has Made $2.2 Million at the First Woman-Run NFT Marketplace". *Fortune*. February 8, 2024. https://fortune.com/crypto/2024/02/07/nft-artwork-woman-run-marketplace-john-le-larisa-barbu/.

Conclusion

"Dr. Rick." Progressive. https://www.progressive.com/commercials-campaigns/dr-rick.

Acknowledgments

First off, none of this would have been possible without my better half, Kevin. Thank you for inducting me into the world of crypto even when I had no idea what I was doing and thought that buying the cryptocurrency XRP in 2019 would be my instant ticket to millions of dollars, an SEC lawsuit notwithstanding. Jokes aside, thank you for always challenging me to take risks and chase dreams. Thank you for your tough love and for always telling it like it is, and most importantly for your patience in me taking time away from our weekends together to toil away in front of the computer to finish this book.

Thank you to my mom for always believing in me in your own way. Thank you for teaching me the value of a dollar, the importance of hard work, and the invaluable mindset that no one owes me anything. Thank you to my dad for sharing with me your insatiable joy of learning, for always being able to treat life with levity, and for always supporting my wildest dreams and letting me learn from my own mistakes. To both of you, thank you for letting me spread my wings halfway across the world even though I know you'd much rather I be closer to home.

Thank you to my brother, Dominic, for being my role model and someone I could look up to my entire life. I don't think I would have studied as hard and got the grades and hence opportunities I did if not for you. Thank you for pursuing the way more sensible career path and giving Mom and Dad two beautiful grandchildren, Danny and Ben, so I don't have to. Thank you to my sister-in-law, Xin Wei, for putting up with my brother, and for showing me what it's like to be a career-minded woman while still being an incredible mother.

Thank you to my best friends who are still friends with me despite having seen me at my lowest. To Janice, you are the most supportive person I know. Thank you for entertaining my incessant Telegram messages and for being someone I can count on at all times of the day. To Pak, your loyalty is second to none. Thank you for being someone I can debate, reminisce, and exchange Instagram Reels about mouthwatering pastries with. To Bryan, Emmanuel, Hann Sern, Kai, Marcus, and Meaghan from my 7Cycle days, all of you are part of my chosen family, and thank you for helping me discover what it's like to truly be loved for me.

Thank you to everyone who works at HUG, starting with Randi who took a chance on a complete stranger you met on Discord and for working with me to build a company that we can both be proud of. Thank you to Alex, our COO and basically my work wife, who is the peanut butter to my jelly and yin to my yang. It is an honor to be breaking the glass ceiling with both of you incredible women every day. To my direct reports Lorr, Tina, Nicole, Michael, and Julia, thank you for living our mission of serving artists every single day, and for embodying the values of diversity and inclusion this space so badly needs. To the rest of our young and lean team – Ken, Amy, Lindsey, Eric, David, Zach, thank you for showing up to work every day with intellectual curiosity and for putting up with all my crazy ideas.

And of course, thank you to the entire community at HUG – whether you were there right from the beginning or have only just come to know of us, you are the reason we get to do what we do.

Together, we are reinventing the future of creative entrepreneurship, and I could not be more excited to see how far we will take each other.

To everyone I've ever worked with at ONE Championship, wow. What a journey we have been on. This may or may not have been the hardest three years of my life, but I did some really cool things, and met the most awesome of people, including my partner of five years and counting. To Chatri – you definitely put me through the ringer, but ultimately made me better for it, saw things in me before I did, and for that, I learned way more than I could have ever imagined. To Ruby, Cedric, Pam, Gaetane, and Shak – thank you for fueling my love for entrepreneurship again. Building one.shop from the ground up is an incredible achievement I will never forget, and I'm sorry I left before we could make it as big as we all knew it could be.

To those I worked with at GIC, thank you for providing me with the best possible start to one's career. Special thank you to Shireesh, who taught me how to lead with kindness, something that I carry with me till today. To Ting, Sean, Debra, Alvin, Darren, Elson, and Jesley, thank you for showing me that work can and should be fun. I'm so proud of how far we've come.

To the city of Los Angeles, thank you for embodying inspiration and joy in both your climate and culture. To the friends I've made in LA and in particular Mark and Allie, thank you for giving me such a warm welcome to the city. It's hard to meet new people and find community in a foreign city, even more so when you are in your mid-30s. To M13, thank you for paving the way to the start of my US career and for helping me open doors to the world of start-ups and venture capital. To Avery and Cristina, you are an inspiration to me. Thank you for constantly encouraging me to lean into my strengths and to lead authentically with unabashed feminine energy.

And of course, thank you to my dog, Guinness. I know you can't read, and you don't really understand anything I say other than "sit" and "stay," but you gave me purpose in some of my darkest days and showed me love that I didn't even know possible. Thank you for being the best dog anyone could hope for.

Finally, thank you to everyone in this crazy Web3 and NFT community, starting first and foremost with all the digital mavericks who agreed to be interviewed for this book. To Zeneca, Jesse, Li, Micah, Claire, Alej, Matt, Jimena, Shavonne, Cozomo, Latashá, Antonius, Larisa, and Randi, thank you for being so candid and sharing your beautiful stories with me. To everyone else, the energy and spirit of this space is infectious and almost hard to put into words, but I'm glad you inspired me to try anyway. Thank you for showing up as your crazy authentic selves. The world may think we are crazy, but we all know we really are the cool kids, because yes – we are still just so damn early.

About the Author

DEBBIE SOON IS a Singaporean investor, entrepreneur, and content creator. She is the cofounder and co-CEO of HUG, an inclusive social marketplace for next-generation creators, launched in 2022 alongside Facebook Live creator Randi Zuckerberg. HUG's mission is to empower creators to become successful entrepreneurs through emerging technologies such as blockchain and AI. The platform supports tens of thousands of creators, enabling them to showcase and sell their work both onchain and offchain. Passionate about bridging the gap between the arts and technology, Debbie is dedicated to using blockchain technology to create more inclusive and fair opportunities for creators. In 2023, she was recognized by nft now as one of 10 trailblazing Asian founders shaping the future of Web3.

Before HUG, Debbie has invested in and built several multimillion-dollar consumer businesses from launch to scale. She was first a portfolio manager for GIC, Singapore's sovereign wealth fund, where she managed over $1 billion in consumer sector investments. She then became chief of staff to the CEO and vice president at ONE Championship, a billion-dollar global sports media property, where she led the company's expansion into new markets and business lines.

Debbie holds a bachelor of arts from the University of Cambridge and a master of science from Columbia University. She also founded Singapore and Southeast Asia's first boutique indoor cycling studio and remains an avid fitness enthusiast today. Outside of breaking down barriers for equitable representation, you will likely find Debbie lifting weights, watching football, or hanging out with her senior dog, Guinness, in her current home of Los Angeles, California.

Index

Page numbers followed by *f* refer to figures.

Accelerate Art, 79
Accountability partners, 140–141
Adamtastic (Adam Paul Levine), 108–109, 108f, 109f
#adversarialEtching, after Modigliani (Sarin), 128
Affirmative action, 178
Aguilera, Christina, 4
AI, *see* Artificial intelligence
AI Art is Not Art collection (Silver), 162
AIM (AOL Instant Messenger), 157–158
Airbnb, 190
Airdrops, 193, 205n2
Akutars, 148
Aku the Moon God, 147–148
Aku World, 143, 147–148
Alcindor, Latashá, 56–61
Alliance Manchester Business School, 182
All Our Faces #2 (Buena Vida), 104f
Allowlist, 106, 204n3
All Time High in the City (XCOPY), 125, 127
Alpha, 106, 115, 204n1
Alpha Centauri Kid, 128
Amazon, 178
Amazon Web Services, 33
America's Next Top Model (TV series), 85, 90
Andreesen Horowitz (a16z), 170, 173–174
Angel check cabal, 106
Anonymity, 132, 156–158, 163
AOL, 73
AOL Instant Messenger (AIM), 157–158
Apollo 11, 202n4
Apple, 11, 19, 42
Appropriation, 162, 206n2

220 INDEX

Aronow, Wylie (Gordon Goner), 135
Art Angels Gallery (Los Angeles, Calif.), 146
Art Blocks, 97
Artbreeder, 160
Artificial intelligence (AI), xiii
   authentication of content and, 75–76
   blockchain to support, 153, 154
   defined, 193
   generative, 152–155, 192
   Claire Silver's collaborations with, 156–163, 164f
   Shavonne Wong on, 155
ArtNet, 21
Arts Council England, 20
Asia's Next Top Model (TV series), 85, 87
a16z, *see* Andreesen Horowitz
Ask Jeeves, 4
Async Art, 147
Atelier Ventures, 170, 174
Atlanta Braves, 143, 145
Atomic Habits (Clear), 134
Authentication, of media content, 75–76
Authenticity, 111, 162
Avenged Sevenfold, 53
Aversano, Justin, 126, 129
Avicii, 71

Balenciaga, 153
Bang & Olufsen, 85
Bankless, 137
Banks, Tyra, 85, 90
Barbie (film), 179
Barbu, Larisa, 181–187
Base, 40, 44–46, 167, 202n3, 203n4

Based (term), 40, 46
BatSoupYum, 127
BAYC, *see* Bored Ape Yacht Club
BCG (Boston Consulting Group), 178, 180
Beauty and the Beast (film), 158
Becoming a digital maverick (process):
   crafting and committing to a ritual, 133–141
   embracing the chaos, 119–124
   getting your hands dirty, 77–82
   identifying your glow stick moment, 49–55
   joining a cabal . . . or making your own, 105–111
   transferring your skills, 91–94
   understanding and holding on to your why, 63–67
   Web3 Toolkit Checklist, 83–84
   your ikigai for, 95–96
Beeple, 101, 107, 128, 152, 190
Betty (@betty_nft), 79, 107, 109, 179
BFAMFAPhD, 20
Bhasin, Roy, *see* Zeneca
Bias, in AI models, 153–154
Bieber, Justin, 135
Big Sean, 58
Big Tech, xv
Billboard, 71
Billboard Dance, 68, 71
Binance, 83, 166
Bitcoin:
   creation of, xvi, 18, 49, 156
   defined, 193
   Ethereum vs., 202n5
   onboarding yourself to, 84
   and other cryptocurrencies, 80
   Jesse Pollack's interest in, 43

sä-v(ə-)rən-tē and donations in, 147
Claire Silver's first investment in, 161
Bitcoin ETFs, 138, 165–167, 194, 206n1
Bitfinex, 43
BitMEX, 43
Black box algorithms, 153, 194
Black History Month, 181
BlackRock, 166
Blade Runner (film), 152
Blender Guru (Andrew Price), 88
The Block (website), 137, 152
Blockchain, xiii
  about, 34–35
  Clubhouse discussions of, 18
  crypto art movement and proliferation of, 130–131
  cryptocurrencies and, 35–36
  defined, 194, 201n1
  experimenting with, 84
  failures of specific, 167
  future applications of, 29
  at HUG, xv
  Micah Johnson on, 147
  Layer 1, 44, 197, 202–203n3
  Layer 2, 44, 131, 167, 197, 202–203n3 (*See also* Base)
  mainstream adoption of, 191–192
  Cozomo de' Medici on, 126
  speculative uses of, 65
  to support AI, 153, 154
  as technology underlying NFTs, 34–35
  validation of, 167
BMW, 108
Bored Ape Yacht Club (BAYC), xiii, 135, 152

Boston Consulting Group (BCG), 178, 180
Boundaries, setting, 135–136
Breaks, taking, 124
Buena Vida, Jimena, 93, 97–103, 104f
Burn mechanism, 120, 121, 194
Burn meta, 121, 194, 205n2
Burnout, 135
Burns, Red, 25
Butcher, Jack, 119–122
Buterin, Vitalik, 202n5
Buzzfeed, 42
Byrne, B., 43

Cabal, 105–111, 123, 139, 191, 194
Calarasi, Romania, 181–182
Calderon, Erick "Snowfro," 97
California Department of Motor Vehicles, 29, 36
Capital One, 172
Carlson, Olaf, 43
Casino Royale (film), 113
CBS Broadcasting Inc., 21
Chainsmokers, 71
Chaos, embracing, 119–124
Chapter 1, I. Birth of Luci (Spratt), 125, 130, 131f
Chapter 3, VII. Wormfood (Spratt), 125, 130
Chase Bank, 57
ChatGPT, 152–154
Checks VV (Butcher), 119–122, 120f
Cherniak, Dmitri, 97
Chicago White Sox, 143–145
Chillicothe Baking Company, 31
Christie's auction house, 74–75, 79, 153, 156
Chromie Squiggles, 97
Churchill, Winston, xv

@ClaireSilver12, *see* Silver, Claire
Clear, James, 134
Clef, 43
Cloud computing, 33
Clubhouse, 17–18, 74, 101, 105
Coinbase, 40, 43–44, 79, 80, 83, 166, 167
Coinbase Pro, 40, 44
Coinbase Wallet, 40, 44, 80
CoinMarketCap, 167
Cold outreach, 89, 139, 148, 173
Collateral, NFTs as, 54
Community, 118, 134, 140–141. *See also* Cabal
ComplexCon, 148
Complex magazine, 40
Connection component, of ritual, 134, 138–140
Consumer applications, Web3, 53–54
Corpo | real collection (Silver), 163, 164*f*
Costco, 57, 178
COVID-19 pandemic:
   adoption of technology during, 18, 26–27
   effects of, 17–18
   hobbies during, 23
   interest in NFTs during, 49, 59
   making art during, 100
   mindfulness practice during, 41
   preventative health initiatives in, 151–152
   Shavonne Wong's 3D art in, 87–88
   Randi Zuckerberg on, 12
"CoZom" (CryptoPunks), 126
@CozomoMedici, *see* Medici, Cozomo de'
Craig, Daniel, 113

Crazy Rich Asians (film), xi
Creativity, xv, 123
Critical thinking, 136
Crypto (game), 52
Crypto art movement, 125–132
Crypto as the how products, 175
Crypto as the why products, 175
Crypto Bahamas, 184
Crypto.com, 80
Crypto companies, Atelier Ventures investments in, 174–175
Crypto Coven, xiv*f*
Cryptocurrency(-ies), xiii, xv. *See also specific types*
   about, 35–36
   blockchain and, 35–36
   defined, 195, 201n2
   failures of specific, 167
   mainstream exposure to, 166–167
   mining, 183, 197
   NFTs and, 36, 80–82, 201n3
   owning and using, 80–82
   Jesse Pollack on, 43–44
   publications on, 137
   Claire Silver's investment in, 161
   skepticism about, 190
   Zeneca's interest in, 114–116, 118
Cryptocurrency exchange (crypto exchange), 79–81, 83–84, 166, 194, 203n1. *See also* FTX (exchange)
Cryptography, 35
Crypto natives, 130, 191, 195, 206n1
CryptoPunks, xiii, 126, 129, 161, 163
Crypto Twitter (CT) community, 88, 115

Crypto whales, 161, 206n1
Cuban, Mark, 178
Custodial wallet, 80, 84, 195, 204n3

Daily Mail, 73
Dall-E, 152
Dapper Labs, 139
Deadfellaz, 79, 107, 179
Dear Evan Hansen (musical), 12
Deathbats Club collection, 53
Decentraland, 203n2
Decentralization, 122, 169, 195
Decentralized application (dApp, dapp), 195, 204n4
Decentralized finance (DeFi), 54, 174, 195
Decentralized social protocol, 195
Decrypt (website), 137
Degenerates (degens), 195, 204n1
DeGods, 179
DEI (diversity, equity, and inclusion) practices, 79, 177–180
Deloitte, 113
Dentsu Aegis, 181
Destiny (Kwon), 125
Digital art movement, 50–51
  artist–collector connection in, 147
  collaborations with AI in, 154, 156–164
  Exchange Art in, 185–186
  Cozomo de' Medici in, 125–132
  NFT Asia in, 88–89
  open edition meta in, 119–121
  self-promotion in, 89–90
DIGITAL fund, 139
Digital maverick(s). *See also* Becoming a digital maverick (process)

Larisa Barbu, 181–187
Jimena Buena Vida, 97–103, 104f
conviction and skepticism for, 167, 169
defined, xiii
DEI practices of, 180
Foodmasku, 23–29, 30f
future of Web3 for, 192
Li Jin, 170–176
Micah Johnson, 143–148
Latashá, 56–61
Cozomo de' Medici, 125–132
Matt Medved, 68–76
Alejandro Navia, 68–76
Jesse Pollack, 40–46
Claire Silver, 156–163, 164f
support for, 190–191
Shavonne Wong, 85–90, 90f
Zeneca, 112–118
Randi Zuckerberg, 7–14
Digital wallet, 166
Discord:
  cabals on, 109
  connecting and reconnecting on, 13, 161
  nefarious links on, 82
  pressure to keep up with messages on, 135
  Web3 community on, xv, 77, 83
  ZenAcademy on, 79, 116, 118
Diversity, equity, and inclusion (DEI) practices, 79, 177–180
Dr. Rick (character), 189
Dot Complicated (Zuckerberg), 11
Duchamp, Marcel, 162, 206n3
Dumb Money (film), 137
Dynamic NFTs, 195, 203n1

EDC Japan festival, 71
Educational component, of ritual, 134, 136–138
El, Laura, 131
Elba, Idris, 85, 89
Elite Daily, 68, 72–73
Elliot, Missy, 61
Empaths (Adamtastic), 108, 108*f*, 109*f*
Enneagram test, 96
Entrepreneurship, 91–92
Equality Lounge, 56
Eras tour, Taylor Swift, 53–54
ERC-20 standard, 205n5
ERC-721 standard, 205n5
ERC-1155 standard, 115, 205n5
ERC-4337 standard, 81, 196, 204n4
ESPN, 113
Eternity (Buena Vida), 103
ETHDenver, 179
Ether (ETH), 196, 206n2
Ethereum:
    Larisa Barbu's mining of, 183
    Base and, 44, 167, 202n3
    Bitcoin vs., 202n5
    crowd sale for, 43
    defined, 195
    and ERC-4337 standard, 81
    Exchange Art support for, 186
    onboarding yourself to, 84
    other cryptocurrencies and, 80
    purchasing NFTs with, 35–36
    Solana vs., 183–184
    Randi Zuckerberg's first experience with, 13
Ethereum ETFs, 166
Eurostar, 181
Everything Everywhere All at Once (film), 170
Exchange Art, 181, 183–185

Exchange-traded funds (ETFs):
    Bitcoin, 138, 165–167, 194, 206n1
    Ethereum, 166
Exhibitions, Exchange Art, 186
Exit liquidity, 106, 107, 137, 196, 204n2
Expectations, managing, 123

Facebook, 5, 7, 9–11, 14, 29. *See also* Meta
Facebook Live, xv, 7, 10
False starts, in Web3, 165–169
Farcaster:
    about, 79
    defined, 196
    Frames on, 168, 175
    Web3 community on, 77, 83
FarCon, 168
Farming tokens, 196, 205n1
Female leaders, in Web3, 178–187
Female Quotient, 56
Ferrera, America, 179
FEWOCiOUS, 130
Fiat currency, 35, 196, 202n1
Fidelity, 166
Field of Dreams (film), 143, 148
Five Instagram Art Accounts to Follow list, 23, 27
Fleseriu, Alex, 183–186
Florence, Italy, 125–126, 132
Foodmasku (Antonius Oki Wiriadjaja), 23–29, 30*f*
Football, 177
Forbes, 152
Forbes 30 Under 30 list, 43, 85, 87
Forbes on Fox (TV series), 10
Fortnite, 203n2
Fortune magazine, 186
Foundation, 28, 174, 175

Founders-in-residence, 151
4chan, 156–161, 163
Frames, Farcaster, 168, 175
Francis, Pope, 153
Friendship, 108–111, 138
Fry, James Richard, 154
FTX (exchange), 81, 152, 184
FTX Ventures, 184
Fungible (term), 35

GameStop short squeeze, 137
Gaming, 51–53
GAN (generative adversarial networks), 128
Ganbreeder, 160
García Martínez, Antonio, 168
Gateway, 74–75
Gehry, Frank, 26
Generative adversarial networks (GAN), 128
Generative AI, 152–155, 192
Generative art, 97–103, 127, 154, 196
Gensler, Gary, 165, 166
Geocities, 4
George Washington University, 70
Gerwig, Greta, 179
Getting your hands dirty, 77–82
Gifted Education Program (GEP), 37
"Glow stick moment," 49–55
Goens, Dee, 60
Goldstone, Nancy, 181
Goner, Gordon (Wylie Aronow), 135
Google, 19, 33
Grant, Adam, 9
Group chats, 107–110
The Guardian, 21
Gun violence, 26

Habits, 134
Hadestown (musical), 12
Hamel, Gary, xiii
Hampshire College, 24
Hands of Time (Kwon), 20
Harare, Zimbabwe, 70
Hard skills, 95
Hardware wallet, 82, 84, 196
Hart, Kevin, 18
The Harvard Crimson, 171
Harvard University, 8, 70–72, 171–172
The Harvard Voice, 171
Health records, 32–34
Heraclitus, 122
Hilton, Paris, 151
Hispanic Heritage Month, 181
Hobbes, Tyler, 97
HODLing (Holding On for Dear Life), 137, 196, 205n3
Hof, Wim, 100
Hopium, 152, 197
Horne, Jacob, 45, 60
HUG (@thehugxyz), 151, 191
  about, xv, 7
  educational programming at, 64–65
  female leadership at, 178
  and Innovation Laboratory, 154
  Tina Survilla Lindell at, 93
  The Medici Collection and, 129
  seed money for, 139
  signing up for accounts at, 83
  X account for, 78
  Randi Zuckerberg and, xv, 7, 13–14
Hundall, Mark, 43
Hysell, Sam, 74

Ikigai, 95–96
"Ilikedat" (Latashá), 59
Inclusiverse, 197
Indiana University, 145
Indonesia, 23–24
Infinite regret, 122
Influencers, 5, 107
Information asymmetry, 107–108
Initial public offering (IPO), Reddit, 156
Inner circle, see Cabal
Innovation Laboratory program, 154
Instagram:
  asking for help in DMs, 101
  Clubhouse vs., 18
  Foodmasku on, 27, 29
  identifying interests on, 96
  Li Jin's art on, 176
  DeeKay Kwon's art on, 19
  Matt Medved on, 74
  Pudgy Penguins on, 191
  Threads and, 153
  in Web2, 5
Interactive Telecommunications Program (ITP), 25
Interests, identifying your, 96
Internet. See also Web1; Web2; Web3
  fear of unknown and, 21, 22f
  history of, 3–6
Interoperability, 168, 197, 206n1
Introductions, 110–111
iPhone, 10–11, 42, 202n4
IPO (initial public offering), Reddit, 156
Italian Renaissance, 125, 126
ITP (Interactive Telecommunications Program), 25

Jackman, Hugh, 11
Japan, 92
JavaScript, 101–102. See also p5.js
Jesperish, 131
Jin, Li, 170–176
Jobs, Steve, 42, 136
Johnson, Demetrious, 92
Johnson, Micah, 143–148
Joydays, 151
JPMorgan, 181–183
The Juilliard School, 8
June Gloom, 201n5

Kahlo, Frida, 129
Kansas City Chiefs, 177
Karkai, Yam, 127
Katya, 25
Kelce, Travis, 177
Kelly, Kevin, 21
Kid Cudi, 130
Kondo, Marie, 67
Kraken, 80, 83
Kwon, DeeKay (DeeKay Motion), 19–20, 22, 125, 127, 128
Kygo, 71

LACMA, see Los Angeles County Museum of Art
Lancôme, 87
Latashá, 56–61
Layer 1 (L1) blockchain, 44, 197, 202–203n3
Layer 2 (L2) blockchain, 44, 131, 167, 197, 202–203n3. See also Base
Leap, 105–107
Ledger, 82, 84
Le Guin, Ursula K., 1
Leto, Jared, 75

Letters from Zeneca (newsletter), 78, 112, 115, 122
Levine, Adam Paul, *see* Adamtastic
Life and Death (Kwon), 125, 128
Lil B, 40
Lindell, Tina Survilla, 93
LinkedIn, 79
LiveJournal, 4
London Marathon, 7
LooksRare, 116
Los Angeles, Calif., 17, 23
Los Angeles Chargers, 177–178
Los Angeles County Museum of Art (LACMA), 78, 129, 156
Los Angeles Dodgers, 143, 145
Louis Vuitton, 24
Love is Love collection (Wong), 90f
Luci collection (Spratt), 125, 130, 131f

M13 firm, 151
McCormick, Packy, 114
McGregor, Conor, 92
McKinsey, 178
Magic Eden, 84, 175
Mainnet, 44
Major League Baseball (MLB), 143–145
Manchester, England, 182
Manikam, Visithra (Vissyarts), 131–132
Marina Bay Sands, xii, xiif
Mason, Kerri, 71
Mastercard, 100, 112
Maximalist (maxi), 169, 197, 206n3
"The Meaning and History of Memes" (*New York Times*), 105
Medici, Cosimo de', 126

Medici, Cozomo de' (@CozomoMedici), 78, 125–132
Medici, Lorenzo de', 125, 126
The Medici Collection, 125–132
Medici Emerging Collection, 129
Medici family, Renaissance-era, 125, 132
Medium, 44
Medved, Matt, 68–76
Memes, 105
Memecoins, 122, 197, 203n1
Meta, 29, 152–153. *See also* Facebook
Metas, 121–122, 167, 197
Metadata, 120, 197
Metamask, 79, 80, 84
Metaverse, 197, 203n2
Michelangelo, 125
Midjourney, 154
Millennials, 3
Milstein, Benjamin (OhhShiny), 139, 167
Mindfulness, 41
Mining cryptocurrency, 183, 197
Minting NFTs:
  by Beeple, 107
  benefits for artists of, 21
  by Jimena Buena Vida, 101–102
  CryptoPunks, 161
  defined, 198, 201n6
  by Latashá, 59–60
  as 1/1s, 121
  and open edition meta, 119–121
  royalties for, 116
  by Claire Silver, 161
  for Shavonne Wong, 88–89
  to your wallet, 80
Mirror, 174, 175

Mr. 703 (art collector), 161, 163
MLB (Major League
    Baseball), 143–145
MLB Network, 146
Modern Luxury, 68
Molnár, Vera, 97–98, 103
MoMA (Museum of
    Modern Art), 161
Monet, Claude, 129
MoonPay, 81, 84
Morpho, 175
Morrison, Jim, 69
Motion, DeeKay, *see* Kwon, DeeKay
MSN Messenger, 4
Mugabe, Robert, 70
Multiverse, 170–171
Murakami, Takashi, 24
Museum of Fine Arts
    (Boston, Mass), 24
Museum of Modern Art
    (MoMA), 161
Music NFTs, 59–60
Musk, Elon, 119, 178

Nakamoto, Satoshi, 43, 156
National Basketball Association
    (NBA), 139
National Football League
    (NFL), 178
National Sawdust, 58
Navia, Alejandro, 68–76
NBA (National Basketball
    Association), 139
Nefarious Meditation (Buena
    Vida), 101–102
Neopets, 52
Netflix, 6, 119, 130
Netz, Luca, 205n4
New Order, 23
New York City, 25

New York Times, 23, 105
New York University (NYU), 25
NFL (National Football
    League), 178
NFT Asia, 89
NFT cabal, 106
NFT finance (NFTFi), 54
NFT Money Flow, 127, 127*f*
nft now (@nftnow), 68, 74–75, 78,
    121, 137, 139
NFT Paris, 179
Nifty Gateway, 84
Nigeria, 70–71
Non-custodial wallet, 79–81, 84,
    198, 204n2
Non-fungible (term), 34, 198
Non-fungible tokens (NFTs),
    xiii–xvi, xiv*f*. *See also*
    Minting NFTs
  AI uses related to, 154
  Aku World collection, 147–148
  for artists, 18–21, 28–29
  author's "glow stick moment"
    with, 50–51
  blockchain technology for, 34–35
  Bored Ape Yacht Club, 135
  bringing up, in conversa-
    tion, 138–139
  Jimena Buena Vida's interest in,
    93, 101
  common examples of, 37–39
  communities built around,
    65, 178–179
  cryptocurrency vs., 201n3
  in *Crypto* game, 52–53
  defined, 198
  as "digital paper," 32–34
  dynamic, 195, 203n1
  on Exchange Art, 183–186
  expertise in, 49

investing in, 136–137
Micah Johnson's interest in, 147
mainstream media on,
    21–22, 137–138
Matt Medved's interest in, 73–74
music, 59–60
purchasing, 36, 80–82, 84
rise of, 17–18
skepticism about, 190
soulbound, 53
token-gating with, 53–54
and traditional gallery
    exhibitions, 131–132
versatility of, 36–39
Zeneca's interest in, 114
Randi Zuckerberg on, 12–13
Non-player characters (NPCs), 6,
    198, 202n1
Normies, 198, 201n4
"A Normie's Guide to Becoming
    a Crypto Person" *(New York
    Magazine)*, xiii–xiv
Northwestern University, 70
Notes app, 67
Now Media, 68, 75–76
NPCs, *see* Non-player characters
Nurturing component, of
    ritual, 134–136
NYU (New York University), 25

Obama, Barack, 10, 11
Oceanic Global, 73
Offchain activities, 202n3
Ogilvy & Mather, 9
OhhShiny (Benjamin
    Milstein), 139, 167
Oklahoma (musical), 12
Onchain activities, 46,
    75–76, 202n2
Onchain Summer, 46

ONE Championship, 92
1/1 artworks, 121, 125, 127
1000 True Fans (Kelly), 21
Only with crypto products, 175
OpenAI, 152
Open edition, 119–121, 198
Open edition meta, 119–121,
    198, 205n1
OpenSea, 84, 116
Optimism Superchain (Optimism
    network), 45, 203n4
Outcomes, focusing on, 123
0xQuit, 166

p5.js, 101–102, 154, 198, 204n2
Paltrow, Gwyneth, 135
Paper, NFTs as "digital," 31–34
Paracosm, 157
Parental introjection, 189–190
Peh, Clara, 88–89
$PEPE, 122
Personality tests, 96
PFP, *see* Profile picture
Phantom, 80, 84, 174
Physical health, 135–136
Picasso, Pablo, 129
PiRIS collection (Fry), 154
Pittsburgh Steelers, 177
Pokemon, 52
Poker, 113–115
Pollack, Jesse, 40–46, 167
Polychain Capital, 43
Polygon, 175
Pomona College, 42
The Pool (Wiriadjaja), 25
Porter, Billy, 87
Portman, Natalie, 9
Pour painting, 159
"Power to the Person"
    (McCormick), 114

Price, Andrew (Blender Guru), 88
Professional athletes, 144–145
Profile picture (PFP), 79,
 198, 203n2
Progressive Insurance, 189
Provenance, 20, 28, 36, 198, 202n1
Pudgy Penguins, 179, 191, 205n4
Pump and dump schemes, 107
Purpose, 95–96

Q-Tip, 58
Quakerism, 41–42
Qualia, 162–163
Queens College, City University
 of New York, 23, 29

Rader, Matthew, 28
Rainbow Wallet, 80, 84
Randi Zuckerberg Means Business
 (radio show), 7
RARI, 101–102
Rarible, 59, 84, 101, 154
RDBMS (relational database
 management system), 3
React, 44
Readymades, 206n3
Reddit, 137, 156
Reddit Collectible Avatars, 38,
 38f, 84
Reed, Pamela, 28
Relational database management
 system (RDBMS), 3
Reum, Carter, 151
Reverse discrimination, 178, 206n1
Revoke.cash, 82
Right-click and Save-As guy
 (XCOPY), 125, 128
Rituals:
 connection component,
 134, 138–140

crafting and committing
 to, 133–141
educational component,
 134, 136–138
nurturing component, 134–136
reassessing, 140
Roberts, Dave, 145
Rock of Ages (musical), 12
Rodgers, Nile, 75
Rohwedder, Otto, 31
Rohwedder Bread Slicer, 31
Roman Empire, 125
Rooney Rule, 178, 180
Rounders (film), 126
Royalties, for NFTs, 116
Rugging (rug pull scam),
 121–122, 199
Runner's World, 7

Safety, Web3, 82, 84
Safronova, xiv–xv, 115
Saint Peter's Basilica (Vatican
 City), 126
Salas, Luisa, 101
Santigold, 61
Sarin, Helena, 128
Sä-v(ə-)rən-tē (Johnson), 147
Scalpers, 203n2
Schroeder, Karl, 149
Schwarzenegger, Arnold, 47
Securities and Exchange
 Commission (SEC, @
 SECGov), 138, 165–166
Seed phrase, 80–82, 199
Self-custodial wallet, *see*
 Non-custodial wallet
Seneca, 115, 118
Sephora, 87
7Cycle, 64, 91–92
The Shed, 58

Shelby and Sandy, 145
Shibuya Crossing (Tokyo, Japan), 129
Shopkick, 172, 173
Silver, Claire (@ClaireSilver12), 79, 127, 156–163, 164f
The Simple Life (TV series), 151
Singapore, xi–xiii, 4–5, 37, 63, 89, 91, 180
Singapore Idol (TV series), 85–86
Sityodtong, Chatri, 92
Skepticism, 190
Skills:
    identifying, 95–96
    transferring, 91–94
SK Telecom, 172
Smart contracts, 29, 154, 199
Snoop Dogg, 132
Snow Crash (Stephenson), 203n2
The Social Dilemma (film), 6
Social media. *See also specific platforms by name*
    building connections over, 139
    Clubhouse vs. other platforms on, 18
    to engage with Web3, 77–79, 83
    ownership of content on, 27–28
The Social Network (film), 10
Social networking, 5
Soft skills, 95
Solana, 36, 84, 180, 183–185, 199
Solomun, 73
Some Asshole (XCOPY), 125, 127
Sonei, Kevin, 93
Sotheby's auction house, 79, 85, 153, 156
Soulbound NFTs, 53
South Africa, 70
Southern Illinois University, 99
Spaces, 105
Spalter, Anne, 101

Spatial intelligence, 37, 37f
Speculation, 107–108, 116, 121–122, 139
Spin, 68, 73
Spratt, Sam, 125, 130, 131f
Stability AI, 154
Starbucks, 38–39, 53
Starbucks Odyssey, 38–39
Start-ups: Silicon Valley (TV series), 11
Stephenson, Neal, 203n2
Stoicism, 118
Subscription services, 119
Support, 111, 123, 190–191
Survivor (TV series), 52
Swift, Taylor, 53–54, 177
Swombat, *see* Tenner, Daniel

TED Conference, 23
Telegram, 83, 109
Tenner, Daniel (Swombat), 31, 34, 36
The Terminator (film), 152
Tezos, 29, 36, 84, 199, 202n2
ThankYouX, 74
Theater Offensive, 25
Threads, 93–94, 152–153, 168
3LAU, 74
333 Club, 112
Three whys framework, 66–67
Ticketmaster, 53–54
TikTok, 5, 17, 27, 40, 96, 125, 153
TIME magazine, 143, 148
Tisch School of the Arts, 25
Token cabal, 106
Token-gating, 53–54
Tomorrowland festival, 71
The Tonight Show (TV series), 108
Topia, 60
Top Shot, 139

Toys R' Us, 108
Transparency, 153
Trezor, 82
Tumblr, 4
Twilio, 43
Twin Flames collection
  (Aversano), 129
Twitter. *See also* X
  Clubhouse vs., 18
  Crypto community on, 88, 115
  Elon Musk's purchase of, 119
  @nftnow on, 74
  in Web2, 5
  Zeneca on, 115
Twitter Blue, 119

Uber, 190
UFC, 92
Uffizi Gallery (Florence, Italy), 126
Uniswap, 175
United Nations General
  Assembly, 29
United Nations SDG Summit, 23
United States Constitution, 32, 33*f*
University of Baltimore, 75
Urban Outfitters, 57

Van der Meer, Durk, 147
Variant, 170, 174–175
Vaynerchuk, Gary, 46, 126
VeeCon, 46
Venice Biennale, 97
Venture capital, 172–173, 178–179
Verizon, 68, 73
Veterans Hospital (Boston,
  Mass.), 25
Vissyarts (Visithra
  Manikam), 131–132
Vogue, 87, 89
Vogue Singapore, 85

Volatility, 65, 102, 122, 175
Vulnerability, 111

WAGMI (we're all gonna
  make it), 167, 199
Walden, Jesse, 174
Wallet Guard, 82, 84
r/wallstreetbets, 137
Warhol, Andy, 162
Warpcast, 83, 168
Washington Post, 153–154
Web1, 3–4, 6, 199
Web2, 3–6, 14, 168, 199
Web3, xiii–xvi
  blockchain as core of, 34
  bringing up, in conversation,
    138–139
  cabals on, 105–111
  co-creation in communities
    of, 64–65
  consumer applications, 53–54
  as cultural movement, 6
  decentralized finance, 54
  defined, 199
  DEI practices for, 177–180
  embracing the chaos of, 119–124
  expertise in, 49
  false starts in, 165–169
  finding your people with,
    110–111
  future applications of, 29, 192
  gaming, 51–53
  getting started with, 102–103
  getting your hands dirty
    with, 77–82
  information asymmetry
    in, 107–108
  Latashá on, 59–61
  mainstream exposure to,
    166–167

mainstream media on, 137–138
memes in, 105
for nft now platform, 75
rituals in, 133–141
seeing the potential of, 49–55
transferable skills in, 91–94
understanding your why for using, 63–67
usability issues with, 81
venture capital investments in, 152
Randi Zuckerberg on, 12–14
Web3 Toolkit Checklist, 83–84
WEF (World Economic Forum), 154
We're all gonna make it (WAGMI), 167, 199
Wesleyan College, 57
West, Kanye, 24, 58
Westworld (TV series), 159–160, 163
WhatsApp, 109
"Why," your:
 cabals based on, 110
 and embracing chaos, 123
 understanding and holding on to your, 63–67, 108, 135–136
Wills, Maury, 145
Winfrey, Oprah, 10, 18
WINK (Women I Need to Know), 109
Winklevoss, Tyler and Cameron, 165
Winklevoss Bitcoin Trust, 165
Wiriadjaja, Antonius Oki (Foodmasku), 23–29, 30*f*
Women I Need to Know (WINK), 109
"Women in Web3" panels, 179–180
Women's History Month, 181
Wong, Shavonne, 85–90, 90*f*, 155

Worldcoin, 175
World Economic Forum (WEF), 154
World Marathon Majors, 7
World of Women, 127
World Wide Web, 4

X (formerly Twitter). *See also* Threads
 author's presence on, xiv
 Bitcoin ETF post on, 165, 166
 cabals on, 109
 discussions of DEI on, 178
 Cozomo de' Medici on, 130
 nefarious links on, 82
 NFT thought leaders on, 49
 noise and discourse on, 66, 134
 pressure to keep up with, 135
 Pudgy Penguin marketing on, 191
 responses to Leap's "cabal" post on, 107
 sharing transferable skills on, 93–94
 Web3 community on, 77, 78, 83
 Shavonne Wong on, 88
XCOPY, 125, 127–128

YouTube, 5, 87–88
Yuga Labs, 135, 139
Yun, Grant, 128

ZenAcademy, 78, 79, 112, 115–118, 117*f*
Zeneca (Roy Bhasin, @Zeneca), 78, 112–118, 122
Zora, 45, 56, 60–61
Zoratopia, 60
Zuckerberg, Mark, 7, 9, 14
Zuckerberg, Randi, xv, 7–15, 94, 112, 139, 151